Out of the Ordinary

the work of John Ronan Architects

Contents

04   **Out of the Ordinary – John Ronan**

08   **Memento Mori**
The Old Post Office

22   **Hybrid Typologies**
Perth Amboy High School

38   **Coming Home**
The Gary Comer Youth Center

56   **Parallel Realities**
Yale Steam Laundry

68   **Shaping a Culture**
Gary Comer College Prep

84   **Brick by Brick, Word by Word – John Ronan**

88   **No Strings Attached**
The Poetry Foundation

118   **Building Blocks**
Erie Elementary Charter School

128   **Civic Engagement – Sean Keller**

134   **The Illusion of Solitude**
Courtyard House

150   **Rooms in Black and White**
Gallery House

162   **The Urban Room**
151 North Franklin

178   **Threading the Needle**
The Ed Kaplan Family Institute for Innovation
and Tech Entrepreneurship

210   **860-880 Lake Shore Drive – John Ronan**

214   **The Spatial Icon**
       University Conference Center

230   **Hope and Optimism**
       The Obama Presidential Center

242   **Wallflower**
       University of Cincinnati Alumni Center

250   **Reflections on the Work of John Ronan – Carlos Jimenez**

256   **That Lost Feeling**
       University College Dublin Future Campus
       and Centre for Creative Design

268   **A Reclaiming**
       Lemont Quarries Adventure Park

278   **Cross-Fertilization**
       Independence Library and Apartments

306   **A Cultural Inherintance**
       Frank Lloyd Wright Home and Studio Museum Learning Center

324   **Dignifying Work**
       Chicago Park District Headquarters

334   **The Next Bauhaus – John Ronan**

338   **Interview**

350   Chronology
354   Biographies
356   Acknowledgements
358   Project Credits
360   Book Credits

Out of the Ordinary

John Ronan

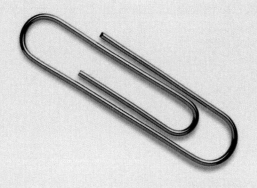

I wish I had designed the common paper clip. For me, this object embodies the essence of good design: it is a response to a functional need in which all the unnecessary elements have been stripped away, leaving only its essential parts in critical dialogue. It is the product of asking ordinary questions about basic concerns, and there is only as much design as is required. Its elegant simplicity is the result of thoughtful, meaningful decisions executed with precision. It feels intuitively correct for its purpose, and there is nothing casual or arbitrary about it. It neither strives to be noticed nor is it about self-expression, and it does not reference its author. The common paper clip, with its appealing, anonymous quality and a timeless character, embodies an important truth: the best design is often invisible, born of ordinary concerns, specific to its task, and hiding in plain sight. The paper clip is the benchmark I use for good design, and its qualities and character are those that I strive to engender in my work.

These qualities are also the hallmark of the best Chicago architecture. If I ask you to name the quintessential Chicago building, you might say the Monadnock Building or one of the masterworks of the early Chicago School, such as the Reliance Building or Carson Pirie Scott. Among other contenders would be Mies van der Rohe's 860-880 Lake Shore Drive or Crown Hall, perhaps Marina City or the Cook County Jail. Then there are the three supertall commercial buildings to consider— the Willis (aka Sears) Tower, the John Hancock Tower, or the Aon building, not coincidentally all named for insurance companies. These architecturally significant structures, emblematic of Chicago's architectural legacy, have something important in common.

They are all ordinary building types.

While other world-class cities are known for their museums, cultural buildings, and monuments, Chicago's reputation rests upon the commonplace building types one finds in any city—office buildings, schools, apartment buildings, department stores. These buildings share a certain straightforward, no-nonsense yet dignified quality—even the jail. On one level, they are eminently practical structures that continue to function for their originally intended purpose. On another level,

5

they transcend the ordinary, becoming icons of place and reflective of their city's values. They *belong* to Chicago, it could be said.

Chicago has always been a tough, no-nonsense place that values hard work, and you can see this reflected in its architecture. Every place has its own DNA, and I would argue that an underlying pragmatism defines Chicago's fundamental character. Unlike coastal cities, the Midwestern capital has no "calling card" industry that demands design and drives culture the way fashion and media do in New York, entertainment does in Los Angeles, or technology in San Francisco. Chicago's value system is informed by staid industries like insurance and financial services, and ever since the early years of the Chicago School, architects who have succeeded here are those who have acknowledged the city's pragmatism while at the same time extracting from it a certain poetry.

I see Chicago as a laboratory in which the commonplace is transformed into the special, and the extraordinary is extracted from the ordinary. This is the architectural legacy and lineage I am honored to be a part of and the lens through which I view my work, searching for the transcendent within the ordinary. Occasionally, I succeed.

2003

Memento Mori
The Old Post Office (2003)

The building was something of a white elephant, built in 1921 and approximately three million square feet in area. A relic of the time when Chicago was the mail-order capital of the world, the structure housed tall stacks of heavy catalogs from Sears and Montgomery Ward waiting to be shipped out across America.

In 2003 I was asked to propose an adaptive reuse for the long-vacant building, which had resisted conversion due its robust structure and gigantic floor plates. A person standing in the middle of one of its vast floors would be 150 feet away from the nearest window. I had come to the realization that the building was essentially a large storage facility, and storage seemed to me still its best use. Knowing that Chicago was running out of open space for cemeteries, I proposed that the building be converted to a municipal mausoleum. Unlike Chicago's famous Graceland Cemetery where the wealthy were buried, this cemetery would be for everyone.

Inspired by Arnold Böcklin's painting *Isle of the Dead*, which shows a shrouded figure and a coffin being rowed to a towering rock with sepulcher-like openings, I imagined funeral barges floating down the Chicago River to the mausoleum. Disembarking at the river's edge, the cortege ascends a ramp to tall, rusted-steel doors that open to a large remembrance hall—once the old post office lobby—lined on one side with funerary chapels. Upstairs, on floors large enough for each one to hold the a decade's worth of burial plots, crypts and niches are stacked six high in a dense configuration reminiscent of Chicago's unvarying street grid. In front of each crypt is a glass reliquary, which, when viewed straight ahead, displays mementos from the personal life of the deceased. When viewed obliquely, the line of glass reliquary fronts dissolves into a single, reflective plane, symbolizing communality and the impartiality of death. To reorient the front of the building from the street to the river, there is a copper-clad building extension on the water side. The raised roadway tunnel that passes through the building's base is clad with thick, rusted-steel plates, recasting it as a memento mori for Loop district commuters.

The white elephant building is a relic of a time when Chicago was the mail-order catalog capital.

Funeral barges transport the deceased
down the Chicago River to the site.

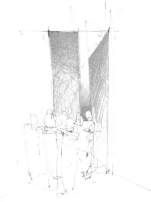

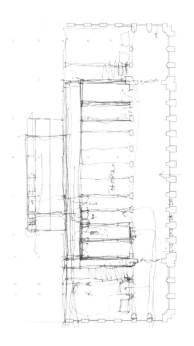

The funeral cortege ascends a ramp to rusting steel doors, which open to reveal a remembrance hall lined with funeral chapels on one side.

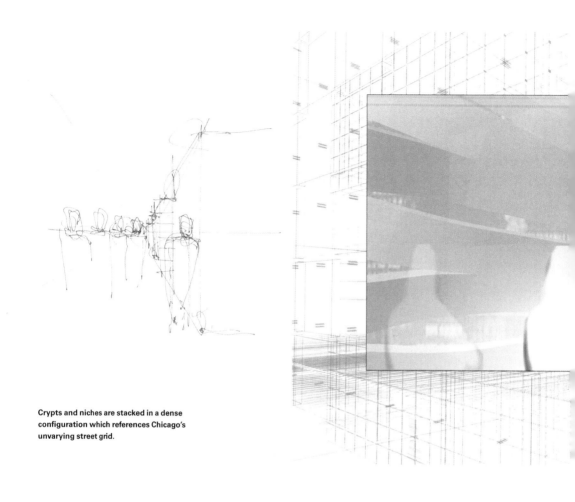

Crypts and niches are stacked in a dense configuration which references Chicago's unvarying street grid.

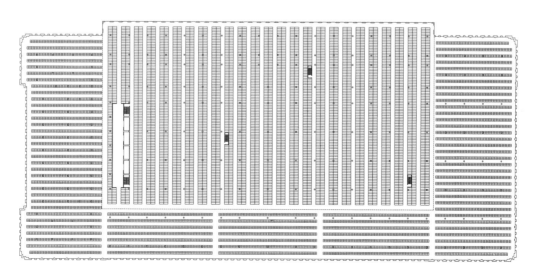

When viewed obliquely, the glass reliquary
fronts dissolve into a single reflective plane.

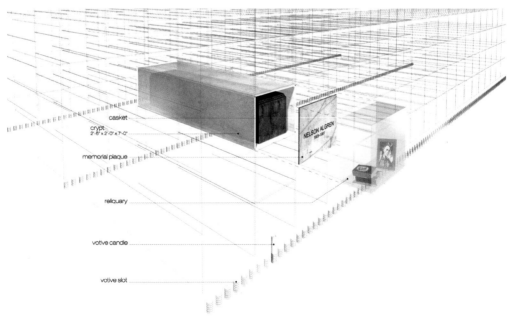

casket

crypt
2'-6" x 2'-0" x 7'-0"

memorial plaque

reliquary

votive candle

votive slot

NELSON ALGREN

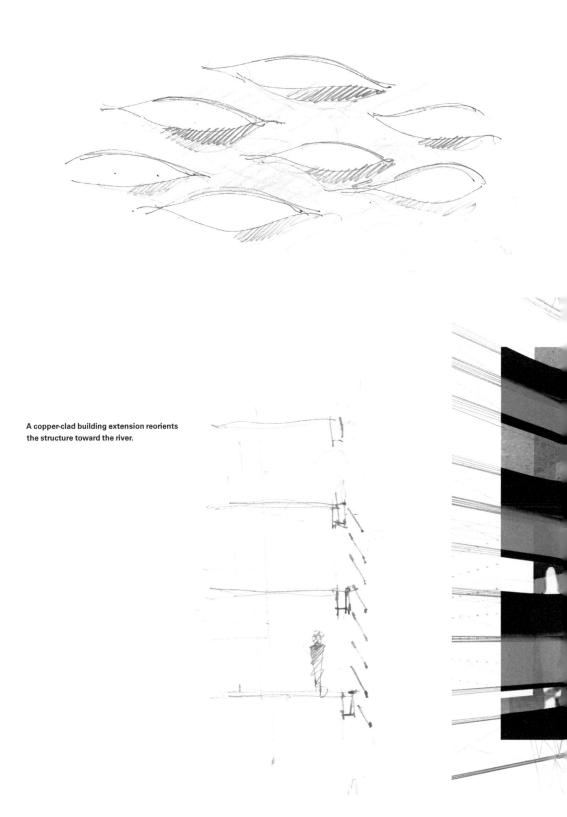

A copper-clad building extension reorients the structure toward the river.

The roadway tunnel passing through
the building's base is clad with rusting-
steel panels.

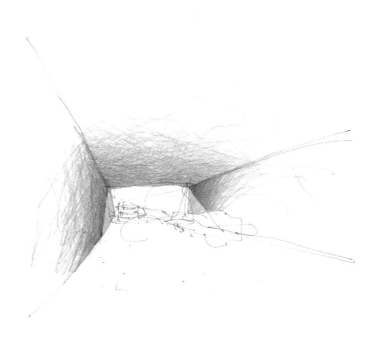

Hybrid Typologies
Perth Amboy High School, New Jersey (2003–04)

Calling it a high school was an understatement. The competition's brief
called for a very large building—almost 500,000 square feet in area.
Given the number of extracurricular programs a school that size could
support, I wondered if it could play bigger role in the community than
a high school usually does. When our firm, along with the three others
in the competition, accepted an invitation to tour Perth Amboy, I saw
a city made up mostly of recent immigrants and underserved by public
institutions. The dearth of libraries, schools, and arts and recreation
facilities led to my decision to design a hybrid institution, part school
and part cultural center, accessible to everyone.

We were the dark-horse competitor, a young firm in Chicago competing
against architectural heavyweights from New York and Los Angeles.
Putting us at further disadvantage, the blind submission process had
been scrapped for in-person presentations, at the request of one of
the famous architects in the competition. The impressive jury included
Harry Cobb, Toshiko Mori, Michael Hays, and Carlos Jimenez.

Standing in front of the sixteen large presentation boards on jury
day, I was as nervous as if I were still in architecture school. I explained
what drew me to the competition: the opportunity to investigate
how communities use their institutions to reinvent themselves,
a phenomenon that intrigued me. I described the critical issues we
had identified and how our proposal addressed them through a hybrid
typology of school and civic cultural center. Our design was not a
building, per se, but the sum of three superimposed systems: the natural
and constructed surface of the site, or the *Mat*; the interconnected
volumes housing the classrooms, which we termed the *Barscape* due
to their linear arrangement; and the *Towers*, which contained the
academic enrichment spaces for the school and the greater community.

We interpreted the site surface as a continuous Mat with different
programmatic zones to support recreation, contemplation, ecology,
outdoor learning, and parking. The natural topography of the site,
which was high on each end and lower in the middle, allowed us to tuck
the parking in the depressed area and place the classroom bars over it.
Classrooms were grouped into one of six learning academies tied

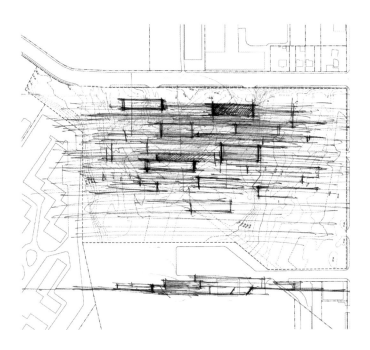

The competition brief called for a very large
building of almost 500,000 square feet.

into the local economy and housed in a flexible arrangement of programmatically indeterminate bars that could be easily reconfigured to meet the school's changing needs over time; the bars could also be expanded at each end to accommodate additional students in the rapidly growing community. This classroom Barscape would be comprised of prefabricated units and craned into place on a platform made of precast concrete double tees spanning the parking lot below; the bars would be discontinuous to allow daylight to penetrate via gratings to the parking area underneath.

Towers housing the programs shared by the school's six academies could be entered from this level or via one of three entry courtyards, internal to the Barscape, to enter the school at the classroom level. The Mat would be surfaced by a porous paving consisting of grass, clay, rubber, or gravel, depending on the programmatic needs of the site.

The spaces shared by the academies—the library/media center, performance hall/ auditorium, fitness/ recreation facilities, cafeteria/ dining, and administration offices—were located in five Towers, whose stacked spaces would also serve as a civic cultural center available to the greater Perth Amboy community. The towers, tall enough to be seen from downtown, were encoded with graphics and color signaling their public nature, inviting the community to participate in the life of the school.

The design competition winner was announced later that night in a ceremony at the local yacht club. I could tell by the nature of the questions the jury had posed that they were intrigued by our scheme, and I was elated when we were announced the winner. Our firm was suddenly "on the map." But the day's excitement was not over. When the car taking me back to the hotel spun out on an icy New Jersey highway, leaving my driver and me staring into oncoming traffic, I was reminded how life can involve sudden reversals in fortune. When government graft drained the pool of funding for public schools in New Jersey, our design was shelved.

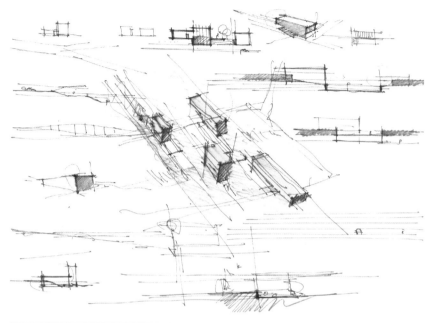

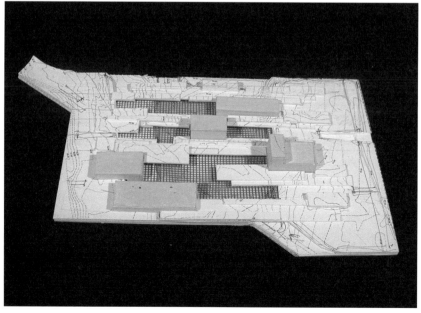

The design was conceived as three
superimposed systems: the site surface
(Mat), the interconnected classroom
volumes (Barscape), and communal spaces
shared by all (Towers).

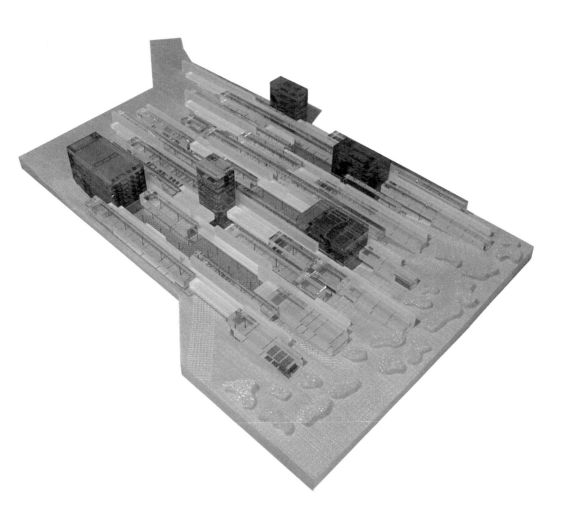

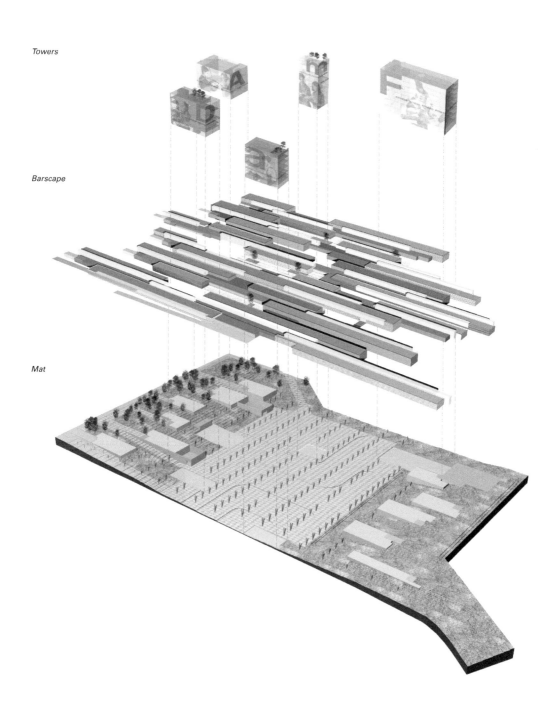

Towers

Barscape

Mat

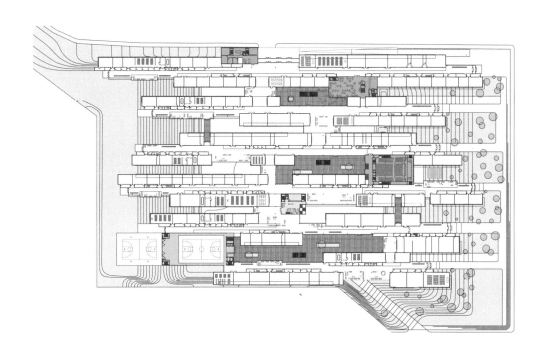

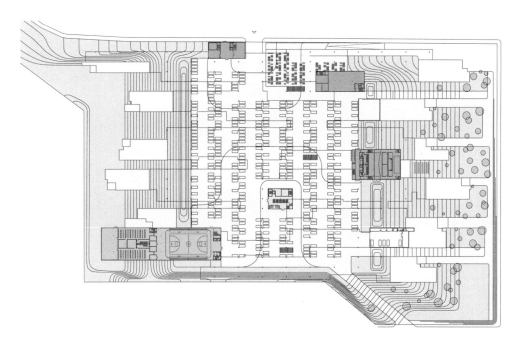

31

The site surface is a continuous mat
supporting ecology, outdoor classrooms,
recreation, contemplation, and parking.

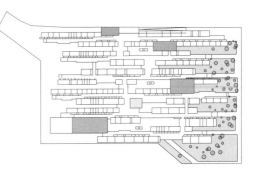

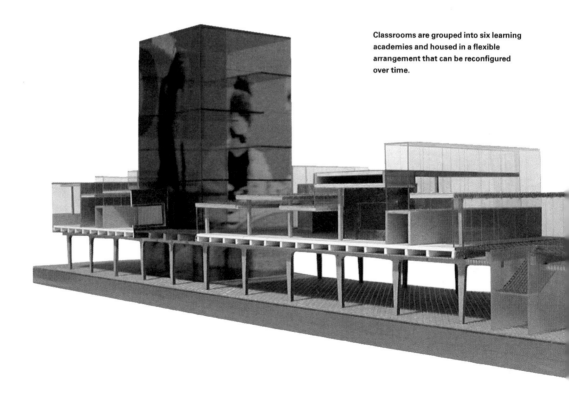

Classrooms are grouped into six learning academies and housed in a flexible arrangement that can be reconfigured over time.

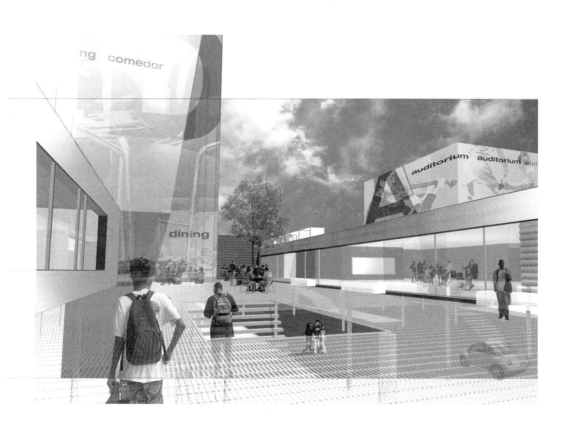

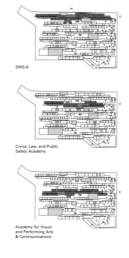

SWS-9

Liberal Arts Academy

Civics, Law, and Public
Safety Academy

Business and Industiral
Information Technology Academy

Academy for Visual
and Performing Arts
& Communications

Academy for Environmental,
Health, and Food Sciences

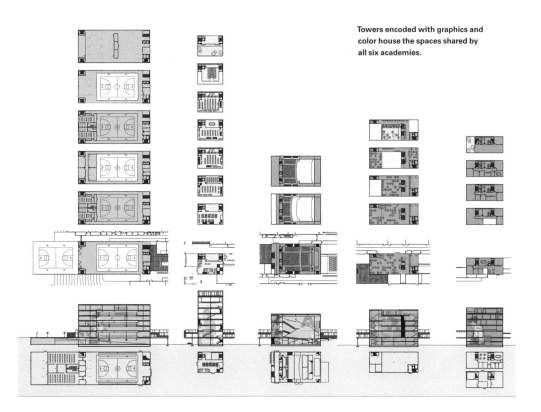

Towers encoded with graphics and color house the spaces shared by all six academies.

37

2006

Coming Home

The Gary Comer Youth Center (2004–06)

The project had a make-believe quality about it from the start.
The unassuming older man in my office, dressed in khakis and a crew-neck sweater, said he was looking for an architect for a small project:
a gym and practice space for a local drill team in Grand Crossing,
a tough, underserved neighborhood on the south side of Chicago.
The drill team was one of the neighborhood's few success stories —
the strict disciplinarian who ran it demanded that team members
maintain good grades and stay out of gangs. The team had nowhere
permanent to practice and had been renting space where they could
find it. My visitor had two stipulations: he wanted the gym to be made
of brick and, because there were so many drive-by shootings in the
neighborhood, the drill team requested it be windowless. All I knew
about my visitor was his name, Gary Comer, so after our meeting,
I looked him up.

I discovered that he was the founder of the Lands' End clothing
company, which had recently been sold to Sears for a staggering sum
of money, making him one of the twenty-five richest Americans.
His idea for the project had been the result of a spontaneous visit to
Grand Crossing, the neighborhood of his youth. What he saw disturbed
him. The neighborhood had fallen into decline, plagued by poverty,
drugs, and gangs. He decided to do something about it by creating
a safe, educational environment for at-risk kids to spend their after-
school hours. The practice gym would be the first step toward realizing
his vision.

What started as a windowless brick gym eventually became The Gary
Comer Youth Center, a four-level, 74,000-square-foot youth education
and recreation center that hosts programs from gardening to dance to
computer graphics. The scope of the project kept growing almost every
time we met. In addition to the drill team practice and performance
space, Gary wanted to provide something for neighborhood kids who
were not on the drill team. "What can we do for them?" he asked me.
Next time we met, I handed him a list of every youth program I could
think of. He took a quick look and said, "Let's do all of these."

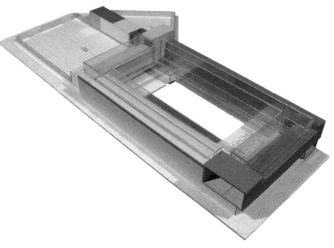

The building form is comprised of four interlocking bars which terminate in important spaces.

We put together the program spaces—art and music rooms, a recording studio, a dance room, a study hall. Gary would call almost daily to add and remove program ideas based on recent conversations. When Gary proposed a health clinic I was dispatched to the University of Chicago medical campus, where I met with a roomful of doctors eager to help. Gary had funded the children's hospital there. The building program was in constant flux, and that fluidity informed its organizational concept. Around the drill team's well-defined practice space we wrapped four levels of programmatically indeterminate "bars" into which we could plug a wide variety of activity areas that could be changed out over time to meet the neighborhood's evolving needs. With adaptability and flexibility the driving concerns, all the spaces would be multi-functional.

Gary had envisioned a theater for the drill team that would be separate from their practice space, but I believed that combining the two was not only possible, but also better for the design. The surrounding spaces would be enlivened by the energy emanating from the activity in the practice/performance space, whereas a separate theater would sit empty when not being used for performances. We designed a telescoping theater-seating system that emerges from a wall under the lobby, and a large stage and proscenium that is revealed by large sliding doors on the wall opposite. Blackout curtains and speakers descend from the ceiling through slots whose flaps open to expose stage lighting. The outdoor spaces are similarly adaptive—the parking lot is a parade-practice ground for the drill team and is a site for community events.

The design is predicated on the concept of spatial layering, the idea being that the user is able to experience multiple spaces and activities from wherever they are. Spatial layering helps create a sense of community. In the case of the youth center, the main gym space can be seen from any room in the building. For example, someone standing near the building entrance is able to see through the cafeteria into the performance space, and then on out to the parade-practice ground/parking lot beyond. And in a building where children outnumber adults by a factor of thirty to one, extended visibility enhances security.

Gary wanted to support Mayor Daley's green roof initiative, so we designed a large roof garden with soil two feet deep where children grow and harvest crops for culinary-arts classes in the ground floor's instructional kitchen. Round skylights in the roof garden bring daylight into the gym and cafeteria below. A tall, metal-mesh tower

is surmounted by an LED screen that announces upcoming events. The sign is visible from the nearby elevated highway, and is a landmark for a neighborhood lacking identity.

Gary's original request for brick was ultimately set aside. The scale was wrong for a building of that size with so few windows, I contended. Instead, we proposed brightly colored fiberglass-reinforced cement panels that reference the uniforms and flags of the drill team, and Gary embraced that alternative. He was adamant that he was building a youth center—not a community center—and the colorful cladding strongly delivered this message. In addition to animating the facade, the variegated pattern of the cladding panels would thwart graffiti. Bullet-resistant glazing protects the children inside areas with large expanses of street-facing glass.

The building design took place over a period of nine months. During the later stages of the process, Gary had a recurrence of the cancer that, this time around, would prove terminal. This alarming news gave a greater urgency to the project, and construction was fast-tracked so that Gary could see the building realized. He died two months after completion. At the end of our last visit together—a tour of the finished building—as we waited in the silent lobby for Gary's car to arrive to take him home, a group of boisterous children, excited looks on their faces, burst from the stairwell, carrying plastic bags filled with what they had just harvested from the roof garden and were taking down to the kitchen. As they stopped to talk to Gary in his wheelchair, proudly showing him the carrots, beans, potatoes, and corn they had grown, I understood that a dream had been realized.

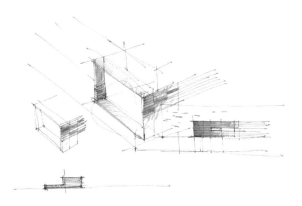

The design is predicated on spatial layering
and the ability of the user to experience
multiple spaces, simultaneously.

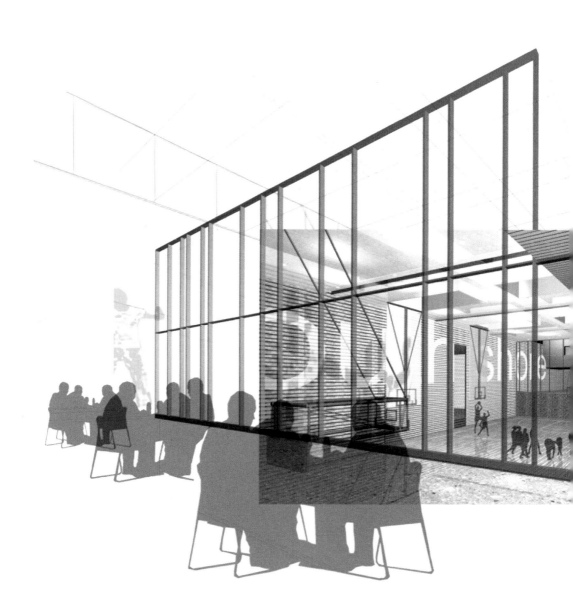

The building's main space is an adaptable gymnasium that can be converted to a 600-seat performance theater.

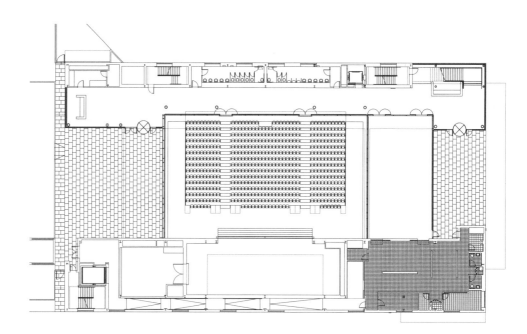

49

A rooftop garden allows children to grow and harvest food crops which are used in culinary arts classes in the teaching kitchen below.

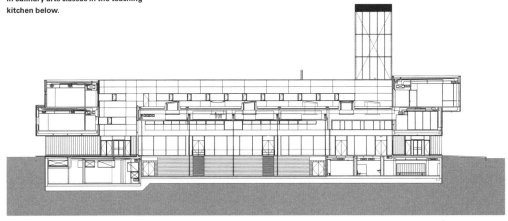

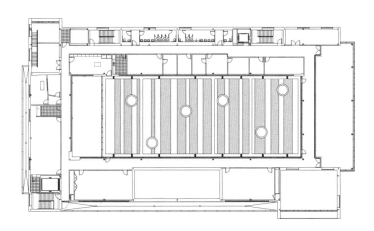

The facade cladding references the drill team uniforms and the variegated pattern animates the facade and thwarts graffiti.

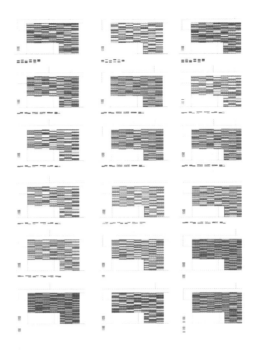

2008

Parallel Realities
Yale Steam Laundry (2005–08)

The most arresting sight in the idiosyncratic building I had been asked to visit was a red scar running like a clay zipper up a glazed-brick interior wall. From the turn of the twentieth century until the mid 1970s, the building had been a commercial laundry where, for low wages, women washed the linens of the White House, Congress, various government buildings, and the city's hotels and restaurants. As I walked through the echoing space, I imagined steam ascending to the vaulted ceilings, clinging to the oddly spaced floor framing, and condensing on its glazed tile walls. This was a building with personality, holding endless stories in its cracked brick and pockmarked concrete walls.

This was one of those projects more about what one *doesn't* do than what one does. In converting the laundry to residential use, it was vital to maintain the distinct character, accreted over time, that originally drew me to it. We identified the "defects" to be retained—holes not to be patched, cracks not to fill, floor and wall damage not to be repaired— and communicated these non-interventions to the construction team in drawings and in building walk-throughs.

As for the necessary requirements of the building's adaptive reuse, we would pursue a design methodology of *select intervention*, surgically inserting elements into the existing structure with an economy of means to convert the building to its new use. We kept new programmatic elements minimal, legible, and discrete. We aimed to create a dialogue between insertions and modifications essential for residential use and the historical structure, with its time-worn masonry shell and quirky floor framing. We would not favor one over the other, but they would co-exist as parallel realities from different time periods.

We chose materials for the new interventions that were sympathetic to the existing structure but had their own personality. Stairs, partitions, and bridge elements made of hot rolled steel plate were inserted into the public areas while maintaining a respectful distance from the building shell. In the residential units, kitchen and bathroom modules encased in Baltic birch millwork were placed like furniture on the worn wood patina of the flooring already in place. New skylights and clerestory glazing brought daylight into the once-dark factory floor.

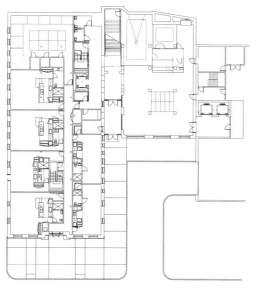

Not everyone found the rich physical history of the building rewarding: the new owner of the apartment with the clay zipper had it covered over with drywall.

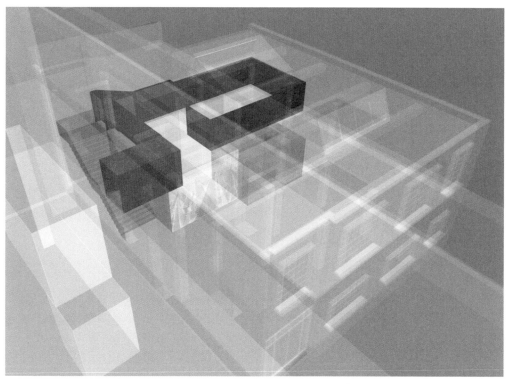

The design pursues a methodology of select intervention, inserting steel and wood elements into the existing masonry shell with an economy of means.

New architectural elements are kept
minimal, legible and discrete.

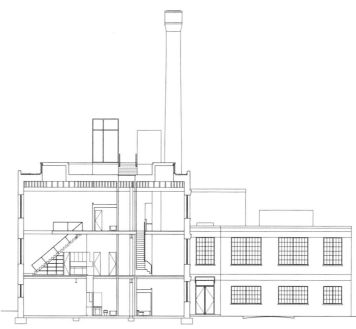

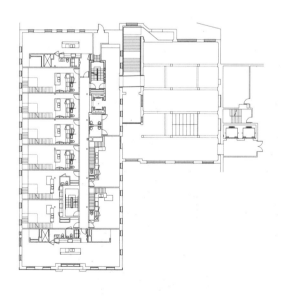

New skylights and clerestory glazing bring
daylight to a once-dark commercial laundry.

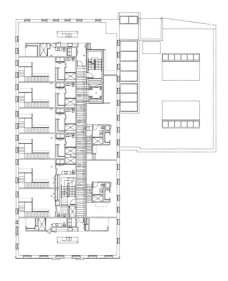

Contemporary insertions in Baltic birch plywood co-exist with the historic masonry shell as parallel realities.

Daylight enters top-floor units via
clerestory glass in the rooftop pool.

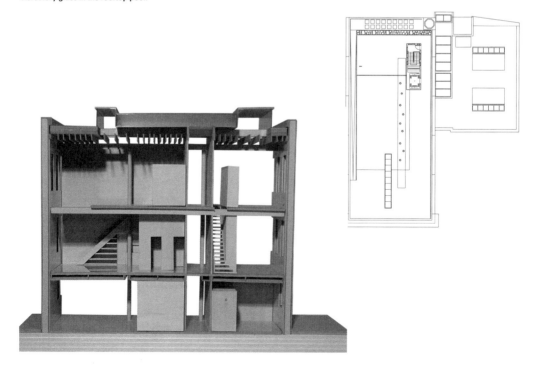

2010

You can't build a reputation
on what you are going to do.
Henry Ford

Shaping a Culture
Gary Comer College Prep (2008–10)

After the tire shop owner agreed to sell, the bar owner was the last holdout. He seemed to be in it for the long haul, hoping out for a big payout. We had no choice but to design around his property and hope he would relent.

To further its educational mission of getting more students in this South Side neighborhood to college, the Comer Family Foundation needed to assemble eleven contiguous land parcels immediately north of the Gary Comer Youth Center (2006) for a charter preparatory high school. The plan was to develop a new building which would leverage the existing youth center, largely vacant during school hours, so that the two buildings could work together as a campus. Classrooms and administrative support would be located in the new building. The adjacent youth center, a short walk away, would house enrichment courses in art and music studios, computer labs, physical fitness facilities, and cafeteria dining.

The project was a sprint from beginning to end. The newly chartered high school was already operating on the third level of the youth center and would soon run out of space by Fall 2010 if the new building wasn't finished. We had a smaller budget than we received for the youth center, but the neighborhood issues of gang-related street violence had not gone away. Unable to afford the bullet-resistant glass we had used on the youth center, we had to get creative. We extended the corrugated stainless-steel siding that fenced in the youth center's the parking lot, and we wrapped it around the facade of the new building. This move bound the two buildings together into an integrated whole and created a protected campus. To thwart drive-by shootings, we perforated the siding that ran in front of the windows, making it hard to see into the building from the street but easy for those inside to see out.

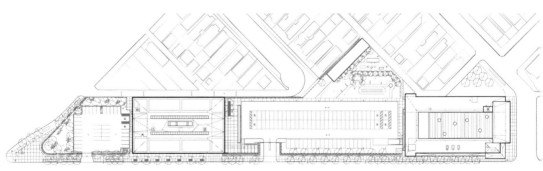

To give the school a distinct visual identity, we clad it in bright green aluminum panels to reference the youth and optimism of the school's faculty, most of whom were recent college graduates in the Teach for America program. To further protect students from street violence, we designed a large movable gate to close off a gathering area away from the street. A double-height glazed lobby space allows views of the adjacent youth center from both levels of the school, and precast concrete pavers surface a walkway between the two buildings

Inside, glass walls between the corridors and the classrooms enhance the school's culture of transparency and accountability. To allow every classroom to receive natural illumination from two directions, we ran skylights along the length of the building, and we separated the second floor from the inner core wall to allow light to filter down to the ground level. Wall graphics highlighting African American achievement designed by the architect both reflect and shape the school's culture.

After being threatened by the city with eminent domain, the tavern owner sold the property during the later stages of construction. The spot where the bar once stood is now the landscaped plaza and gathering space that students named The Quad.

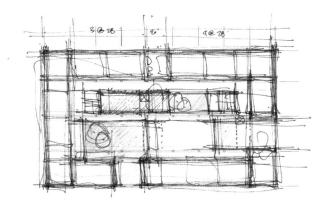

The stainless steel fence which surrounds
the property becomes the building facade.

The perforated metal cladding makes it difficult to see into the building during the day and easy to view out, to address security concerns.

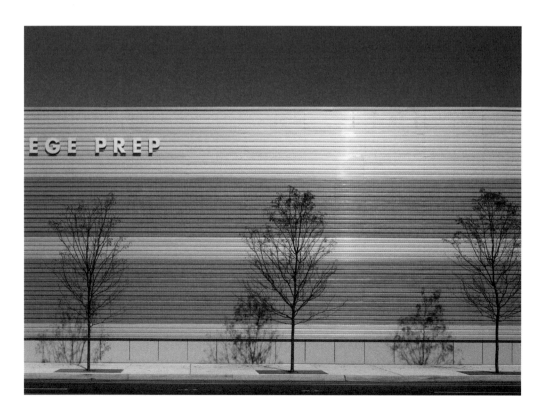

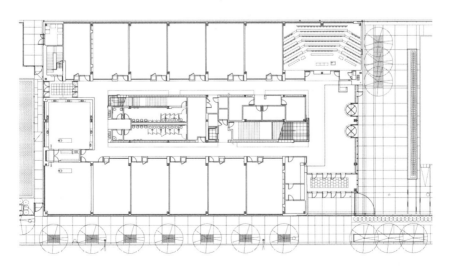

Skylights running the length of the building
bring daylight into corridors on both levels.

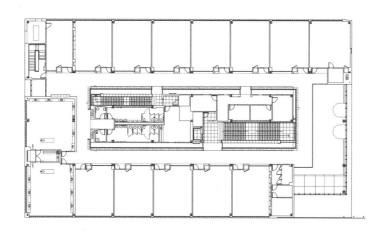

Glass corridor walls bring daylight from
two directions into each classroom,
and support a culture of transparency
and accountability.

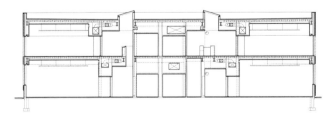

Architect-designed wall graphics
highlighting African-American achievement
both reflect and shape school culture.

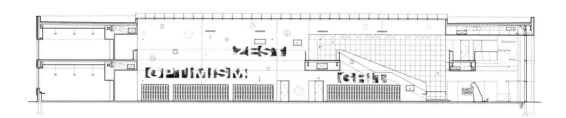

Brick by Brick, Word by Word

John Ronan

I make my living as an architect and one of my favorite buildings is a poem. It was constructed in 1966 by Seamus Heaney and I make periodic return visits to it and, like any great work of architecture, I find something new each time. Like the best buildings, it provides a memorable experience which touches all the senses. When Heaney describes "Under my window, a clean rasping sound/When the spade sinks into the gravelly ground," I can hear the sound of shovel hitting gravel. And when he writes about new potatoes, "Loving the cool hardness in our hands," my own hand involuntarily contracts as my sense of touch is activated. Likewise, I can smell "the cold smell of potato mould" in my nose, while the onomatopoeia of Heaney's "the squelch and slap/Of soggy peat" transports me to a bog in my subconscious. And when he describes his grandfather pausing his back-breaking work to drink bottled milk, I taste it, too. Through language, he creates a three-dimensional space that I can inhabit, and his observations and memories beckon me to enter.

Heaney constructs his poem like a skilled mason using common brick. As he builds the poem word by word, what becomes so striking is the shear ordinary-ness of both its subject and language. Heaney doesn't resort to inventing words (though who knew a "drill" was a furrow?); when he writes "between my finger and my thumb/The squat pen rests; snug as a gun," even a kid can understand it. Through the precise selection and controlled arrangement of words, the common act of digging in an Irish peat bog is made extra-ordinary, and the mundane becomes transcendent. This use of commonplace language makes the poem's architecture all the more impressive, and sends us the reassuring (yet somewhat intimidating) message: Look, it's all there hiding in plain sight.

Heaney situates his poem carefully, creating what architects like to call "a sense of place," resisting generic recall when he claims, "My grandfather cut more turf in a day/Than any other man on Toner's Bog." He describes not just any bog, but a specific place which his language invites us to imagine (substitute "the" for "Toner's" and see how the atmosphere changes). In a subtle and deft act of transference, his deeply-rooted memories become ours.

I often ask myself, why does this poem stick in my head? What makes it special? The conclusion I have come to is that, like all great works of art, it endeavors not to be noticed, but to be *remembered.* And to succeed in being memorable something must make an *emotional* connection. Heaney achieves this with an impressive economy of means, in eight short stanzas constructing a space for us to inhabit and inviting us in; a place with its own smells, sights, sounds, tastes, and textures. As his pen digs into the past, the palpable admiration he describes for his father and grandfather—despite their different paths in life—begins to register, causing us to think about our own relationships, our own choices. Heaney's work is personal, but not about self-expression (which would exclude us). It has its own order and form like a memorable piece of architecture, its beginning and end slightly asymmetrical but purposely so.

> But I've no spade to follow men like them.
> Between my fingers and my thumb
> The squat pen rests.
> I'll dig with it.
> —From *Digging,* by Seamus Heaney

We are all poets, Heaney seems to imply, and just as he digs with his pen, for us it is a matter of finding an instrument through which to find our own voice. As an architect, I write with wood, concrete, glass, and metal, calling attention to those things that are in plain sight but hard to see. In my line of work, materials are the words, buildings the poem. And just as the Heaney crafts poetry through the careful selection and ordering of words, I endeavor to thoughtfully select and arrange materials in a way that creates authentic experiences with which people form meaningful bonds. If I am doing my job correctly, the building will unfold space by space like a poem unfolds line by line, and each visit will yield new discoveries. Like Heaney, I am conscious of those who came before me and whose legacy I extend. In my case, it is skilled Chicago architects from a tough, no-nonsense town which values hard work, but who managed to transcend pragmatism and extract a certain poetry from it. Their digging is what I see when I look out the window of my office (by God, they could handle a spade, too). I follow in their path, planting in their drills, searching for the transcendent within the pragmatic. Occasionally I succeed, and the building becomes a poem.

This essay was originally published in the March 2018 issue of *Poetry* magazine.

2011

No Strings Attached
The Poetry Foundation (2007–11)

I wanted the project for the Poetry Foundation to cut against the grain of contemporary architectural design. It would be about relationships, not form; about the experience, not the image. In my opinion, too much of contemporary architecture was about getting noticed, rather than about creating something that will be remembered, like a piece of literature that rewards each rereading. I didn't want it to shock or surprise but to unfold slowly, space by space, as a poem unfolds line by line, to gradually draw visitors into a world that rewards close attention.

The Poetry Foundation project began like a fairy tale: an elderly reclusive heiress, Ruth Lilly, gifted a small fortune to the seat-of-the-pants organization that had published the highly respected *Poetry* magazine since 1912. The most unusual aspect of Lilly's gift was that she placed no stipulations on its use. The magazine was free to do with the money what it chose, with no strings attached. Gifts of this size typically come with restrictions on its use, but Ms. Lilly made none.

In response to the gift, the Poetry Foundation was formed, and its board decided to create a "home" for poetry that would include a library, performance space, exhibition gallery, offices, and a garden. There was no paradigm for a building of this kind, unlike there is for, say, a school or a house, which meant we were embarking on a journey into the unknown. The garden space, because it was an unusual requirement, seemed like a good point to begin generating the design. Various strategies for combining a garden and building, such as knotting, overlapping, interlocking, etc., were explored in diagrams; these ideas were in turn tested on the site through hand sketches and sketch models. The concept that emerged was that of a garden created through the erosion of an implied volume as described by the boundary of the L-shaped site. In this way, the garden would become another "room" of the building, internal to its organization and integral to its programs.

The foundation's board struggled over the question of how public the building should be. Some felt admission should be granted only after making a formal request, while other board members wanted it to be readily accessible to everyone. Our design mined this tension by placing the entrance to the building itself away from the street. To reach the door,

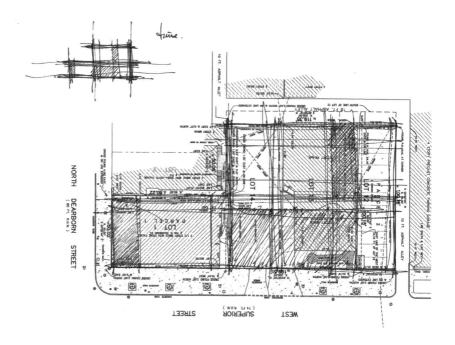

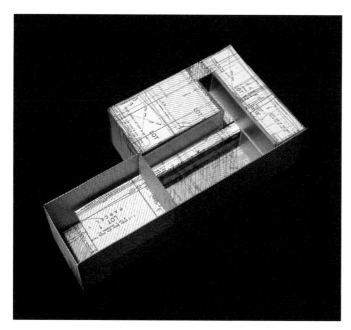

Initial studies explored a garden space created through the erosion of an implied volume described by the site's L-shaped boundary.

visitors have to walk through the garden, a space that would create a deliberate ambiguity about public and private. Anyone who was willing, or intrigued enough, to take the journey could come in. This outdoor room would mediate between the street and the enclosed building. It would be a shared urban space belonging simultaneously to the institution and the city.

To enter this urban garden room, you ascend two steps from the sidewalk, a subtle change in elevation that slows you down, signals removal, and gives a sense of entering another world. Immediately upon climbing the steps, you find yourself in a narrow passageway with an undulating glass curtain wall compressing the space. The material layers come close together and new relations are created: one can see the reflection of the screen wall on the opposing glass wall. Once inside the garden proper, the double-height library comes into view, announcing to visitors that they are entering a literary environment. Popular with casual visitors and neighbors, this outdoor room operates as something of an urban sanctuary, a place of reflection and quiet contemplation where the distractions of modern life are stripped away. Bounded by its perforated-zinc street wall, visitors are a part of the city but removed from it at the same time.

The building was conceived not as an object but as a series of independent tectonic layers—in wood, glass, and metal—that converge and separate in a deliberate way to construct the building's spatial narrative. What results is what we call a building but is actually the manifestation of the overlap and interplay of these layers. No layer is all that interesting itself. The spatial complexity resides in the how the layers change according to the viewer's perspective.

The intention was to start with ordinary materials—concrete, plywood, corrugated metal—and make them transcendent or special in some way, akin to the way a poet selects and arranges ordinary words to create something new, to make language strange in a way that causes us to rethink what we thought we understood or to uncover a truth. The task of the architect is likewise not so much one of invention, but that of arranging the space-defining elements in meaningful yet unexpected ways.

Having decided to use concrete to surface the ground floor and garden, we experimented with this humble material to transform it into something special. We started with the stone, looking at over fifty different combinations of aggregate before settling on the right mix and size of the stones. To finalize the recipe, we investigated different sands, cements, and admixtures (or their omission) in an iterative process that involved hundreds of samples. Once the final mix was determined, we experimented with various levels of sandblasting, done by hand, to achieve the right texture. A full-size mockup was created on site to test the mix and to assess the details we would encounter. This entire investigation, which took months, was conducted by the architect in partnership with a local concrete contractor whose knowledge of the material was critical to our success.

We conducted the same iterative process with the other materials. Birch plywood was selected for the wood layer because of its strength— it had to support library books—as well as for its humble status and its natural character. We chose zinc for the corrugated metal screen wall because of its purity, reflecting poetry's elevated standing as an art form. To transcend its industrial origins, we oxidized the zinc to turn it black, connoting both authority—the color of judges and priests' robes or a black belt in martial arts—due not only to *Poetry* magazine's authoritative status in the literary world but also to imbue the building with an enigmatic, mysterious quality. The black corrugated metal veil-like facade gives the structure a certain ambiguous quality—its ordinary industrial cladding is strange in an urban context—and allows glimpses from the street into the layered spaces inside.

The diaphanous qualities of the screen wall depend upon viewing angle and light conditions. Seen obliquely, the building looks monolithic and solid; viewed frontally, the screen wall becomes transparent. Sunlight on the screen wall gives it more presence in the daytime, while at night it seems to dissolve and become more recessive, allowing the artificially lit garden and interior spaces to become more dominant.

The objective in designing the Poetry Foundation was to create a serene, calm environment in which people enjoy spending time. Like literature and poetry, it uses language to tell a story, but is not *about* language. It's about communication, not self-expression. It is an invitation, with no strings attached.

The screen-enclosed garden space is an
outdoor room which mediates between
the building interior and the street.

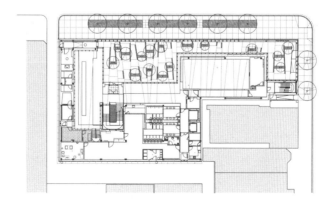

A narrow passage leads to the garden,
where the library comes into view,
announcing to visitors that they are
entering a literary environment.

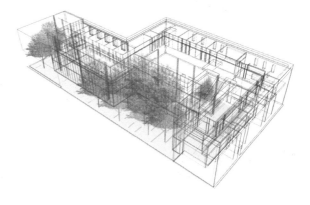

Bookshelves in Baltic birch encircle the
building in a continuous ribbon.

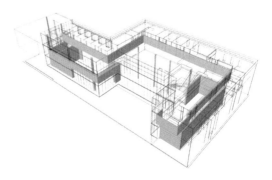

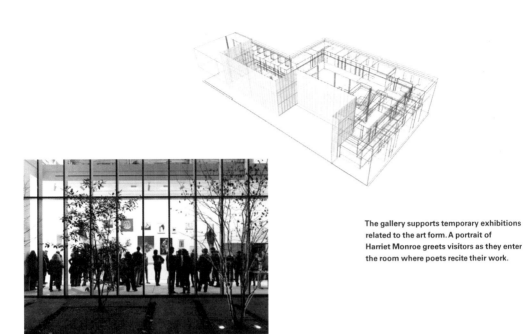

The gallery supports temporary exhibitions related to the art form. A portrait of Harriet Monroe greets visitors as they enter the room where poets recite their work.

In the performance space, poets recite their work against the backdrop of the garden and library.

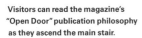
Visitors can read the magazine's
"Open Door" publication philosophy
as they ascend the main stair.

The second floor office level offers views
through the garden.

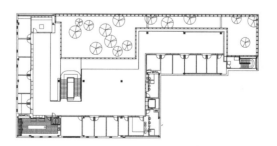

112

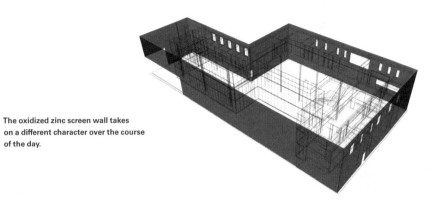

The oxidized zinc screen wall takes on a different character over the course of the day.

113

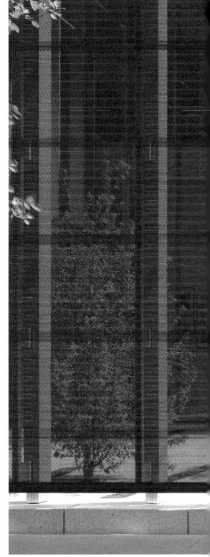

When viewed obliquely, the building
appears solid and monolithic, but becomes
transparent when viewed frontally.

2013

Building Blocks
Erie Elementary Charter School (2011–13)

The school board had come to us in search of a new identity for the charter school they had founded six years earlier. Erie Elementary was operating out of a building, originally constructed in 1960 as a Catholic school that had all the telltale traits of school architecture from the post-war era: the alternating bands of ribbon windows and yellow brick, the glass blocks. The successful, predominantly Spanish-speaking charter school had outgrown that structure and needed a gym, playground, elevator, additional classrooms, and administrative support space. The board hoped that the new addition would become the main entrance and would offer a new visual identity in keeping with the school's mission of preparing students for a diverse global society.

To make room for the addition, we needed to demolish an existing convent on site. The new building would have to connect into the existing structure at each level, which is normally not a problem, but the old building's closely spaced floors—only nine feet apart, vertically—posed some challenges, causing us to orient the mechanical runs vertically rather than horizontally. Even more challenging was the budget, which was so bare bones that it came to drive every design decision.

One of those decisions was the exterior wall material. We started with what I knew to be the least expensive material to enclose the building— precast concrete. Often relegated to warehouses and industrial structures, we endeavored to elevate it to an institutional level the school would be proud of. After researching the largest panel sizes we could fabricate and get to the site, we proposed an exterior wall of large, colorful precast panels stacked like children's blocks to lend a playfulness befitting an elementary school. The two-story-tall concrete panels make the building a learning tool, its stacked tectonic expression explaining the way loads are carried to the ground in a way that even a child can understand. To make this ordinary building component feel special, we hired a terrazzo contractor to grind and polish the panels at the factory, giving them a shiny and almost luxurious appearance which imbued this ordinary material with a simple yet noble character. We chose panel colors that play off those of the existing structure and surrounding residential buildings.

119

On the primary street facade, we set the elevator core back to create a new school entry perpendicular to the face of the building. The new double-height lobby and signage tower gave the school a monumental and dignified quality. Inside, the program spaces are stacked in a manner similar to the precast cladding of the building exterior. A gymnasium and recreation room on the third level are stacked over the library, classroom, and computer-lab spaces on the first two floors. Large windows between the precast panels speak to openness and transparency, inviting the neighborhood to participate in the life of the school.

The compressed urban site forced us to locate the playground on the roof, where it has views into the gym below and is visible from the street through a large aperture on the building's primary facade, making the students an integral part of the school's new identity.

The rooftop playground has views to the gym below and the neighborhood beyond.

Colorful precast concrete facade panels
are stacked liked children's blocks.

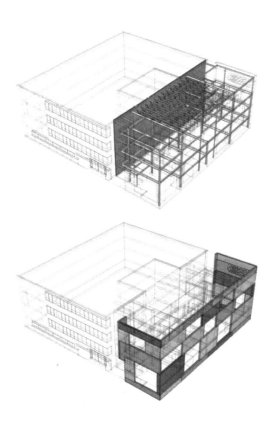

Precast concrete facade panels are
ground and polished to give them
a special character.

Civic Engagement
Sean Keller

John Ronan's buildings demonstrate what civic architecture in the United States can be today. Which is to say they have been designed and built in a context that often challenges the very possibility of civic spaces and civic life. As the site of most of his work so far, Chicago plays a familiar role here as the paradigmatic American city—as a city of extreme contrasts: of economic and racial inequity, of raw free-marketeering and energetic public action, of architectural greatness and urban degradation. As an architect devoted to the fullness of the city, Ronan works with unusual skill across these polarities, bringing excellence not only to expected sites, such as the Poetry Foundation and an office tower in the Loop, but also, and more impressively, to the tough neighborhoods in which the Gary Comer Youth Center and the Independence Library and Apartments are located.

Ronan's projects create significant civic spaces not by avoiding, but by working with, these challenging conditions. What registers in the resulting buildings are thoughtful assemblies of space and material, but we should keep in mind that this handling of architecture's traditional materials is possible only because it is matched by an equally adroit handling of the entire architectural process, from initial conversations to completed construction. Both are guided by Ronan's persistent, and democratic, belief in the equality of dignity: that all of our cities' places and people are equally deserving of great design. (Need it be said that this is not—or should not be—a political position? It should be the basis of architecture's claim to be a profession.)

Public architecture—or architecture with a public aspect— pushes this process far beyond anything as simple as an architect-client relationship. Instead, these buildings are the material evidence of sprawling constellations of individuals and organizations—public and private—drawn from across a city that has many divisions. Such constellations do not spontaneously emerge, and they certainly do not automatically produce good buildings. Success demands the skills of an architect who can balance leadership and collaboration, stubbornness and compromise, vision and pragmatism. It requires an architect who practices civically.

As Ronan's body of work shows, the goal of this relentless collaboration is the creation of mature, compelling architecture of world-class quality. Here it is worth noting that, if there is a generally international feel to his buildings, that may largely be because the standards of design and construction that his projects achieve are today more commonly seen outside of the U.S. than domestically. One mark of his practice's success is that it manages to realize such high quality under the more challenging conditions of the current U.S. building environment. His buildings should serve as a provocation for a more vital strand of such high quality public architecture in the U.S. It would be a mark of great progress if, one day, more buildings met the mark he has set for the profession and its clients.

However, we should be clear about the sources of this achievement. Over the last half century many ambitious architects—especially those, like Ronan, with academic affiliations at U.S. universities—seem to have decided that buildings themselves were not enough. In order to be intellectually or politically relevant, architecture, it seemed, needed to be supplemented with something else: with critical theory or computation or urbanism or ecology. Intellectually it has been a great ride; and as a way out of certain blinkered aspects of modernist thinking and designing, this expansion of the field has had some benefits. But it has also dramatically weakened the disciplinary expertise of architects, and precisely at a time when the profession is already being pushed to the margins of the building process by owners representatives, financial partners, and large construction firms.

In contrast, Ronan has made a characteristic choice to remain focused on the building, and his portfolio presents a compelling argument for the benefits this clarity of focus. Within the hothouse of academia this may appear to be conservative position, but in its real impact in the city it is anything but. (It would be another matter if his practice did not have the range it has; if, like so many, he designed only for the wealthy.) Rather than theatrically political gestures, Ronan creates thoughtful buildings for citizens, regardless of their politics (or income or ethnicity). By attending carefully to its own concerns, his architecture thereby becomes a model for good citizenship—it demonstrates and embodies what it means to be responsible, to have good judgment, to consider others. In this way a building can also become an intellectual project in itself, rather than a diagram of concepts borrowed from elsewhere.

Here it is helpful to compare this attitude to that of Ronan's predecessor at the Illinois Institute of Technology, Ludwig Mies van der Rohe, who so stubbornly tried to divorce architecture from politics. Taking a position that seems increasingly shameful, Mies sought to isolate architecture first from the blinding intensity of interwar German politics and then from the racial exploitation that remade Chicago's Southside in the postwar period. In doing so he provided a model for the architect as a politically detached genius concerned only with timeless issues of form, beauty, and truth. (There were worse cases: see Philip Johnson.) That this was always only one aspect of Mies mattered little when this high-minded detachment from politics was quickly debased into the spinelessness of a thousand corporate hacks.

Needless to say, Ronan's emphasis on the building itself, and on architecture as a discipline itself, does not lead to the same destination. For unlike Mies, his approach is not exclusionary, but immersive, embedded in the communities for whom he works. (His aesthetics also are not exclusionary; more on that below.) Because of this real engagement there is no need to add politics before or after design, and the building itself becomes a refined, yet pragmatic, response to its social context. In this way Ronan works in a way that is more Chicagoan, more American, than Mies, not surprisingly, ever did.

Ronan's approach should also push us to recognize that contemporary buildings are already complex artifacts, not only in their planning, but in the myriad specialized technical systems that they require. While a careful handling of materials is certainly essential to his work—especially in the more refined cases of the Poetry Foundation and the houses—it is really building systems, such as structure, exterior cladding, glazing, and interior finishes, that are the elements of his palette. Ronan deploys these systems and their interactions to define and sequence spaces as a resolution of a building's program and site.

Here again there is an important distinction to be made within the broad similarity to Mies's approach. When formulating an architecture—and a school—on the basis of material primitives (brick, wood, steel, glass, concrete), the midcentury master pushed his building elements toward complete exposure. Though the realization was not always complete, the drive was always for each element to be visually complete and undifferentiated in itself before being added together to form an assembly such as a facade or a stair. We can see this platonic mindset as the ultimate source of the entwined aesthetic success and practical shortcomings of Mies's buildings. This reductive drive left no place for the realities of modern buildings—no place for ductwork, pipes, and cables—and gave little space for the realities of reality—of rain, snow, heat, cold, wind, and

131

sound. (A good symptom of the trouble this caused are Mies's ceiling/roof assemblies, which proved to be the most difficult building planes to resolve.)

In comparison, Ronan wisely accepts many of the givens of contemporary construction and use, and then orchestrates these into compelling architecture. The resulting practice is thus more open and adaptable, with specific solutions found in each circumstance. The critical issues around energy and climate are fully integrated— actualities that Mies and many of his generation largely ignored in their pursuit of a new aesthetic. The most extreme demonstration of this revised attitude is in the Innovation Center that Ronan has designed for the Mies-dominated campus of IIT. While clearly recalling the skin-and-bones architecture of the neighboring Mies buildings, the Innovation Center offers a contrast not only in tonality—white to Mies's near-black—but in the fundamental conception of what a building is. Ronan's building takes all of the HVAC systems that Mies seemed to wish away and makes them essential. The building's non-iconic iconic facade *is* a heating and cooling (and lighting) system. Its inflated ETFE cushions are actively adjusted in response to the weather (which Mies also imagined away), dispelling the modernist fiction of isolated and unvarying materials. Instead, Ronan sees the building as a composition of material and energy systems sympathetically interacting with its fluctuating environment.

Avoiding any fundamentalism of materials also allows Ronan to make the most of situations in which use and/or budget require materials that are not obviously "noble" in themselves. Smartly handled at the Poetry Foundation, honed concrete makes a better connection to its urban context than travertine or terrazzo (Mies's exterior use of the former in Chicago was always absurd). In the Independence Library and Apartments, careful detailing of corners and good daylighting make a double-height wall of concrete block noble rather than bleak (an old lesson of Brutalism).

This open approach to materials also allows for the most dramatic departure from anything Miesian: the happy use of vivid color combinations in Ronan's schools and the library. Taking a tip from Robert Venturi—who is also form-checked in the LED sign tower of the Gary Comer Youth Center—Ronan has taken advantage of the inexpensive, but incredibly effective, sphere of expression provided by large-scale color. (Here we might remember that the supposedly hard-nosed Bauhaus had a vigorous program of wall-painting.) Architects do not think of color as a material, but many building materials are artificially colored—and, as in clothing, the less expensive the building, the more artificial color one finds. With a characteristic combination of pragmatism and attunement to context, Ronan converts the necessary choice of color into large-scale fields that give a strong, anchoring, presence to these projects within neighborhoods that have been wracked by economic and social disruption.

Importantly, this vibrancy is always in support of the buildings' users and their communities, never at their expense. In his writing and designs, Ronan has clearly rejected the formal contortions that mark much showpiece architecture today. The basis for this decision can be traced back to a historically parallel argument made more than a century ago by Adolph Loos in his (in)famous critique of the excesses of Secessionists. While some of Loos's reasoning may now strike us as misguided (or worse) there is one quite compelling argument that lay at the base of his position. The overwrought *gesamtkunstwerk* projects of the Secessionists were, in Loos's view, smothering in their totalizing aesthetic. Misunderstanding the role of architecture, they left no room for the lives of their inhabitants. Instead, as Loos demonstrated in his own designs, buildings should be seen as platforms or stages providing spaces within which their occupants can play out their lives, with their own props, without being dominated by the formal obsessions of an architect.

Translated into a contemporary vocabulary, Ronan's buildings take a similar attitude. When architects (and architectural critics) talk about "organizing spatial sequences," they are emphasizing a purely aesthetic concern for abstract, empty volumes—which is surely a legitimate part of the discipline. But we should never lose sight of the fact that, in actual, occupied buildings, these sequences are not just relationships of space, but also of people. What Ronan creates—with far more openness than Loos—are layered stages on which the major or minor stories of civic life can play out, with the architecture supporting these dramas. All of his compositions grow out of this point of view, whether the long, multilayered view through the Comer Youth Center; the sectional connection from the sidewalk through the Independence Library; the more complex revelations of the Poetry Center, passing from street noise to reading room stillness. In an era that is increasingly fractured, it is an architecture that believes in the potential of buildings to offer open-ended connections between people—to provide compelling spaces within which we can play out our many roles as citizens of a democracy.

133

2017

The Illusion of Solitude
Courtyard House (2013–17)

The site was never the same from year to year. The winter wind coming off Lake Michigan blew the sand into unpredictable hills and valleys, and a new rock-walled harbor entrance to the south prevented the sand from sweeping back into the lake, lengthening the distance between the street and the shore with each passing year. As the beach got bigger, so did the houses. New Hamptons-style homes were constructed, inching ever closer to the receding waterline as the sands became longer with time. Amidst two such structures we would build a house to offer the owner that rare luxury, the illusion of solitude.

The house is a spatial composition of four outdoor courtyards in dialogue with the interior rooms. Its materials are informed by the locale: burnt driftwood, which references beach bonfires; sandblasted glass, to echo beach glass made translucent by the waves; stone; and water. One steps up from a large, flat boulder into the entry courtyard and proceeds across a bridge spanning a reflecting pool, a tree at its center. A double-height living space offers views of the lakeside courtyard and, beyond it, the water and a nearby lighthouse. A dining courtyard, east of the kitchen, receives morning sunlight but is shaded in the late afternoon. On the south side of the house, a small courtyard with an outdoor shower is oriented toward the beach. Each of the four courtyards serve as light monitors and are strategically screened from adjacent properties to preserve the feeling of isolation and privacy.

Over time, as westerly winds hurl sand at the house, it, too, will change, increasingly taking on the worn appearance of the driftwood found scattered among the sands that inspired it.

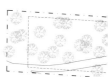

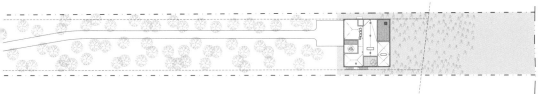

137

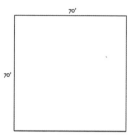

70'

70'

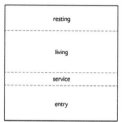

resting

living

service

entry

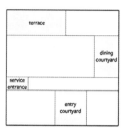

terrace

dining
courtyard

service
entrance

entry
courtyard

The house is organized in four zones, each
with an outdoor courtyard space.

The home's four courtyard's each have
a unique materiality and character.

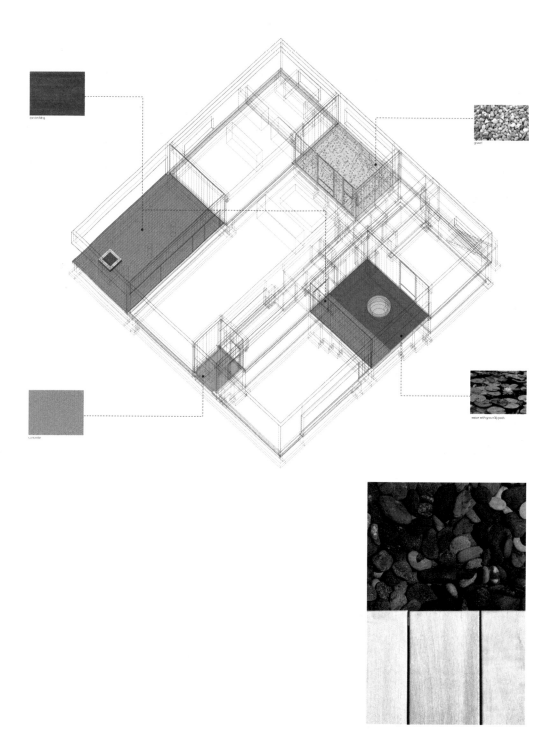

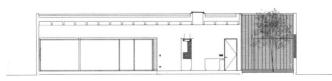

Walls of cast glass admit daylight while preserving privacy. Windows are located to frame views of the nearby lighthouse and lake shore.

147

148

2017

Rooms in Black and White
Gallery House (2015–17)

After an extended tour of the owner's museum-quality collection
of black and white photography and hearing him extoll the nuances
of Eugène Atget, I was firmly in agreement with Walker Evans' opinion
that "color photography is vulgar." The reduced palette of black, white,
and gray in the photos has a clarifying effect and serves to focus the
viewer's attention on composition and content. Besides, I'd always been
predisposed to palette reduction. But how might this collection inform
the house design, which I now understood would need to be at least
as much gallery as home?

We would eschew the open planning which has dominated residential
design for decades in favor of a collection of discrete gallery-rooms.
The black-and-white prints would be displayed in the four masonry
volumes that comprised the house and in the gallery-like interstitial
spaces linking them. A reduced material palette was carefully selected
to serve as a backdrop for the collection, and colors were introduced
that would not upset the subtle balance of the work on display
throughout the home.

The photos would speak, the architecture would listen.

We had a special brick made for the interior and exterior walls—
warm gray in tone and two feet long, laid up in a random bond to
suppress repetition. It gives the house a timeless, elemental character.
Steel-framed sashes in large masonry openings suggest apertures
more than windows. The cast-glass planks that filter the daylight in the
gallery-like hallways between rooms have a low iron content to remove
any green-colored tint and render the glass as neutral as possible in
tone. We continued the gray slate used on the entry walkway and front
porch through the gallery spaces of the house like a stone carpet and
back out again to the rear terrace, which feels like an outdoor room
due to the longwise positioning of the garage. Projecting bricks on
the garage's terrace-facing wall cast long dark shadows onto the warm
gray wall in the late afternoon sun.

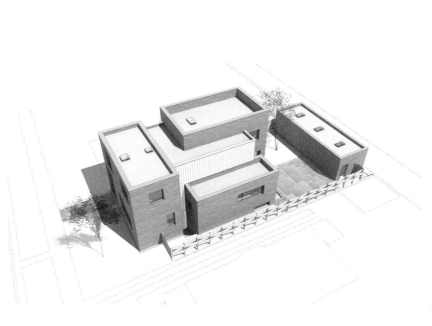

Steel-framed openings in the facade
suggest apertures more than windows.

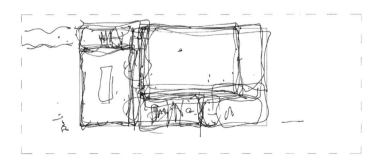

Gallery-like interstitial spaces connect
the masonry volumes which comprise
the living spaces.

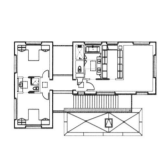

2018

The Urban Room
151 North Franklin (2012–18)

Animals instinctively avoid pain, so I don't often work for developers. However, I couldn't resist the invitation to do my first high-rise building—a speculative office tower—on a site in the Loop financial district. The site was not ideal—a block away from Wacker Drive, where the newest Class A office towers were being built along the river. In addition, our 36-story tower would be surrounded by taller existing structures.

Most buildings of this typology are formal exercises, but our approach was driven by urbanism. The idea was to establish relationships between the spaces of our building and the surrounding streetscape and its view corridors. To accomplish this, we carved out the base of the building and turned the resulting space into a three-stories-tall covered public outdoor plaza, extending an adjacent park space into the site. We raised the plaza only slightly, so it would still feel part of the street. This urban room was designed to mediate between the building interior and the city, the same way that the Poetry Foundation garden mediates between the enclosed building and the street, only here it does so at a much larger scale. The plaza, with the café that opens onto it, was intended to create a unique spatial condition in the Loop: a privately owned public outdoor setting for working, gathering, eating, and relaxing.

The lobby entrance is accessed through the plaza, and large windows in the sandblasted mirror-clad elevator core strengthen the connection between the outdoor and indoor spaces. There are two ground-floor lobby lounges, one sunken and one gently raised, each out of the main traffic flow. The grand stair in the raised lounge leads up to the more casual second-floor lounge that overlooks the lobby and is adjacent to an outdoor terrace, which we created by sliding the office floors above it to the property's western edge. In contrast to the dynamic activity of the plaza, the upper terrace has the contemplative atmosphere of a pocket park. Direct sunlight at noon makes it a popular lunch spot, and throughout the day its zen-like atmosphere draws workers on laptops. An open stair connects this space directly to the street, acknowledging it as public and completing a continuous sequence of interconnected indoor and outdoor lounges that start with the street-side entry plaza.

163

At the roof level we placed another outdoor lounge space, exclusively for tenants, with views of the city skyline.

The interconnected indoor and outdoor lounge spaces were designed to acknowledge new modes of working and to allow employees to gravitate to the environment in which they feel the most comfortable and productive. At the time, companies were trying to shoehorn as many people as possible on a floor to reduce real estate costs, and technology was enabling a more mobile work force. These two factors combined to make the building's outdoor lounges serve as a kind of release valve, allowing workers to leave the office without leaving the building.

Our plan was to have the tower floors housed in a single, strong, clear volume with a taut glass skin. This smooth glass slab would appear white from the outside and, together with its rounded corners, would give the building a light, clean, technical appearance—like a white iPhone—and be in contrast with the carved stone character of the lobby. We made ceiling heights in the office tower ten feet high to maximize daylight, and the air conditioning was controlled floor-by-floor to increase energy efficiency.

The end result was only a partial success. Our idea of an interconnected series of indoor and outdoor public spaces in dialogue with the city around it was realized, but the building's iPhone-like wrapper was abandoned in favor of a more economical curtain wall, a decision we were informed about only after the fact. An overheated construction market had forced the developer to cut costs somewhere, and they chose to take it out of the tower's hide. "The budget is the boss," the developer unapologetically explained.

A speculative office tower is something to be filled with rent-paying tenants and then sold as an asset. Essentially, it's a financial instrument made of stone, steel and glass. Agreeing to participate in its development was essentially a transaction, which begins to explain the dispassionate attitude of everyone involved in the process—everyone that is, with the exception of the architect.

The urbanism-driven project seeks to establish critical relationships with the surrounding urban context.

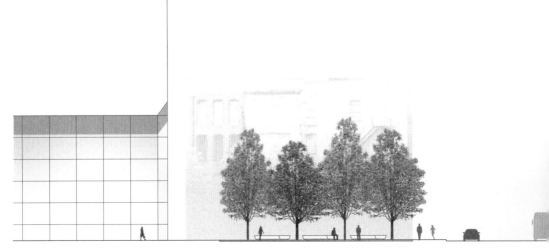

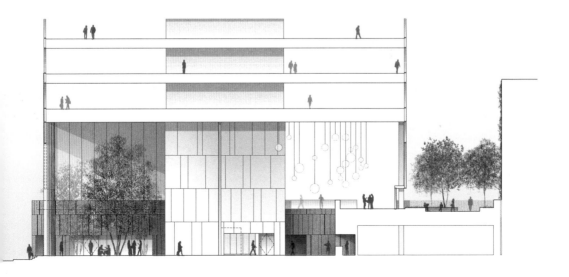

The lobby space clad with jet mist granite
feels hallowed out from a solid stone block.

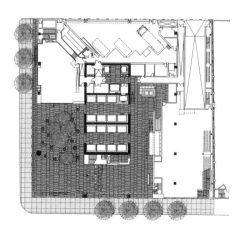

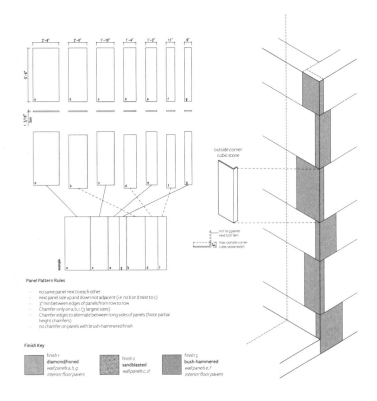

2'-8" 2'-0" 1'-10" 1'-4" 1'-2" 11" 9"

5'-4"

1 3/16" / 3cm

a b c d e f g

example

outside corner cubic stone

no f or g panels next to 6" dim

max. outside corner cubic stone width

Panel Pattern Rules

- no same panel next to each other
- next panel size up and down not adjacent (i.e. no b or d next to c)
- 3" min between edges of panels from row to row
- Chamfer only on a, b, c (3 largest sizes)
- Chamfer edges to alternate between long sides of panels (Note partial height chamfers)
- no chamfer on panels with brush-hammered finish

Finish Key

finish 1
diamond/honed
wall panels a, b, g
interior floor pavers

finish 2
sandblasted
wall panels c, d

finish 3
bush-hammered
wall panels e, f
interior floor pavers

Stone slabs are cut into seven cladding panel sizes for more forgiving construction tolerances and to eliminate waste.

Elevator core walls of mirrored sandblasted glass reference melting ice.

The upper terrace has the contemplative
atmosphere of a pocket park.

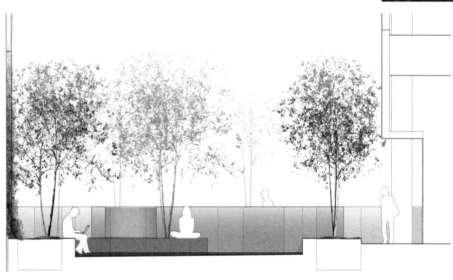

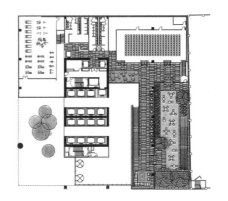

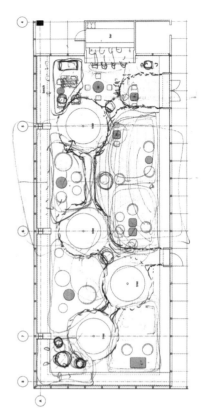

2018

Threading the Needle
The Ed Kaplan Family Institute for Innovation
and Tech Entrepreneurship (2014–18)

"It's like a clear Teflon," the university president said. "You see, this is Teflon," he continued, as he sketched out the chemical formula. "If I add one molecule, I get ethylene tetrafluoroethylene"—the material commonly known as ETFE. I had proposed using that fluorine-based polymer as the cladding for the Kaplan Institute, the innovation hub my firm was designing on the campus of the Illinois Institute of Technology. I was concerned that the university might react negatively to a material relatively new to architecture. ETFE, which was developed originally for the sails of racing sailboats, had yet to be put to architectural use in Chicago. But if anyone was going to be receptive to the idea, it would be the two men I was meeting with: the university president, a chemical engineer by training, and the provost, had a PhD in material science. They were not intimidated by technology, and they wanted a forward-looking building. Their engineering background helped them understand the idea and quickly embrace it.

We had been asked to thread the needle with this project. On one hand, the building needed to be inventive if it was going to reflect its purpose as host to project-based courses in innovation and entrepreneurship. On the other hand, we were given a budget more appropriate for building a high school than a university facility. Innovation is notoriously expensive; the ordinary much less so since it's been done countless times. Our project had to be both innovative *and* cheap. When the staggering figures for the glass enclosure we initially proposed arrived, I had to think about less costly alternatives. Mies had described Crown Hall as "skin and bones" architecture, and I wanted to carry on that tradition, but using materials that were not available to Mies. The ETFE was a lightweight material, a tiny fraction of the weight of glass and less costly. It was relatively new to architecture and would give the building a weightless, cloud-like appearance. It also represented a Gottfried Semper-like return to origins that I thought was appropriate for where higher education now found itself.

The first school was started under a tree, by someone who came to be known as a "teacher" talking with young people, who came to be known as "students." This dialogue was the origin of our university system,

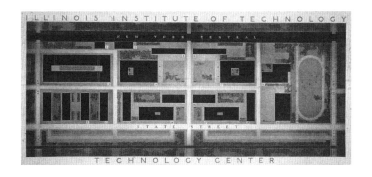

which for centuries has been the place where knowledge resides and is transferred; however, the world is changing. These days, knowledge is readily accessible to anyone with a computer connection, and creativity and entrepreneurial initiative the keys to success and so the role of the university must change along with it. While knowledge and skills were once all that was needed to advance in one's chosen career, today creativity and entrepreneurial initiative are the keys to success. It's no longer about what you know, but about *what you can do* with what you know that matters, and universities were now in the business of developing a student's ability to adapt to changing conditions in an increasingly competitive career environment. University buildings must also evolve to reflect this new reality, and we would use the innovation center project to explore this possibility. We were asked to design what would be less a classroom building than an *idea factory*—a place of creative interaction between students and faculty across disciplines, where new ideas are explored and tested on their way to becoming meaningful innovations.

I had been teaching at IIT for some time and was frustrated with the lack of a destination outdoor space on campus, where block-like classroom buildings sat on a carpet of green with only residual space between them. We conceived of the innovation center as a hybrid of building and campus space, organized around open-air courtyards which function as outdoor classrooms and provide the outdoor destination spaces the campus currently lacked, but first, we would need to find a site.

We settled on a site in the center of campus, aligned with the library and with the original student center to the south, both similarly scaled buildings. The location, which had once been a parking lot and was now covered with sod, was ringed with mature ash trees that had succumbed to an emerald ash-borer infestation; we cut them down and used their wood in custom-designed furniture for the building.

Another challenge was to make our inventive building feel "at home" on the campus designed by Ludwig Mies van der Rohe, one of the masters of the modern movement. Mies's campus was planned on a 24-foot grid and had three distinct types of structures: classrooms, laboratories, and communal buildings that were intended for use by the entire university community, like the library and student center. The Kaplan Institute would combine all three types—a new kind of classroom building and laboratory for ideas for use by everyone.

181

The cantilevered second level provides sun
shading for the recessed glazing below.

We started by testing the 24-foot organizational grid that the campus is based on to determine its validity today. We asked faculty at the Institute of Design, which would be occupying the building's second floor, to sketch out their preferred classroom setup. We then tested these layouts against the grid and found that it still held up, so we adopted it. The building's 24' × 48' bay structure conforms to the underlying campus grid, but, in a departure from the black painted steel used all over campus, we painted the structure white. I wanted the Kaplan Institute to be more welcoming and user-friendly than Mies's stern black-steel and buff-brick classroom buildings. Students might spend all day in our building, so it was important that it be an airy and comfortable environment. We punctuated the white interior here and there with color, adopting the palette of Post-it notes, which are commonly used in human-centered design courses like those that would be taught in the building. The color scheme suggests, in a subtle way, that ideas are vital to the building.

The floor plan is organized around two landscaped open-air courtyards. Visitors enter the building through the courtyards, which serve as destination outdoor meeting spaces otherwise lacking on campus. The courtyards are connected on the building's second level via a covered passage; this allows people to walk through the building without ever going inside. The courtyards' two-story glazed walls allow natural light to penetrate deep into the floor plate, making the interior bright even on Chicago's gloomiest winter days. Courtyard landscaping provides building users with a continuous connection with nature and supports the storm water management strategy: roofs slope to a perimeter gutter at each courtyard, and rain is conducted down into the gravel floor via rain chains, where it is slowly released into the city sewer.

The first floor of the building includes studio space, state-of-the-art maker space, and a café which serves as a university crossroads to promote collaboration and chance encounters. The floor plan configuration mimics the design process, allowing students to move fluidly between different modes of thinking and making in a recursive way. Large horizontal floor plates are open to allow visual connection to multiple spaces at one time. Openings in the floor plate provide views from floor to floor, fostering the sense that the building is a single collaborative community. Spaces are flexible and adaptable, with furniture and walls that can be reconfigured easily. Project and meeting

spaces requiring sound isolation are enclosed with demountable partitions so they can be rearranged as needs change.

The second floor, home to the Institute of Design, cantilevers over the ground floor to provide sun shading and is enclosed in a dynamic facade of the ETFE foil cushions. Sophisticated pneumatics make it possible to vary the amount of solar energy entering the building through these cushions, moving their four layers of foil together and apart in real time in response to changes in weather and daylight conditions. The ETFE foil is one percent the weight of glass and gives the building a light, cloud-like appearance. My goal was make Mies's Crown Hall—which I consider to be very lightweight for its time—look heavy in comparison to our building, which appears ready to float away if not tethered to the ground. Being on the second floor feels like being inside a cloud, apart from sections of clear glazing open to views of the two internal courtyards.

Building systems are technologically advanced. Water-filled plastic tubing embedded in the concrete-filled metal floor decks converts the structure into a radiant heating and cooling system, an idea that Mies would have admired. How a wall turns the corner was an important to Mies and also to Schinkel before him; the IIT campus is a compendium of modernist approaches to this question. Our solution was to wrap the ETFE around a transparent, solid acrylic rod at each of the building's corners in order to enhance the lightweight appearance.

I happened to be on campus the day the ETFE showed up on site— the entire facade in a single wood crate, measuring 4' × 4' × 24', on the back of a semi-trailer truck. Watching it installed in the following days, and seeing it inflated, I knew that we had threaded the needle.

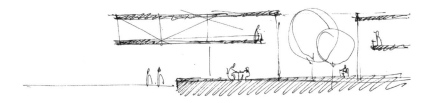

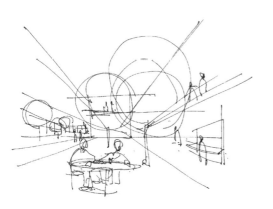

The building is organized around two open-air courtyards through which visitors enter the building.

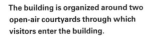

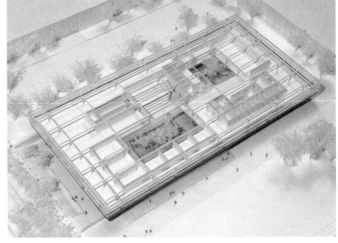

Metal chains conduct rain water from a permiter gutter to the gravel courtyard surface below.

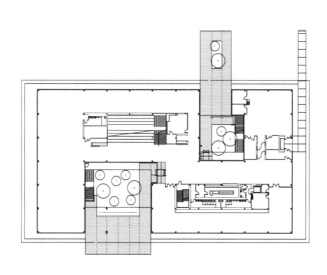

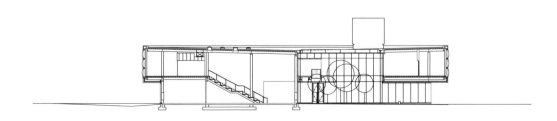

Collaboration spaces support fluid
movement between different modes
of thinking and making.

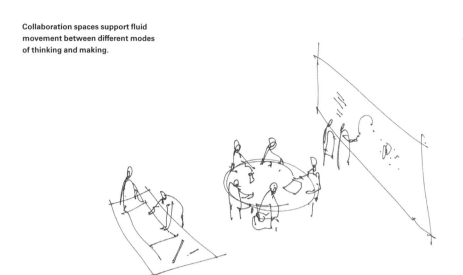

Maker spaces are visible from the main
pathway through campus.

Courtyards are connected via a covered
passage at the second level, allowing
people to pass through the site without
entering the building.

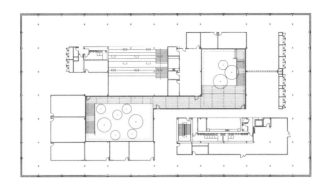

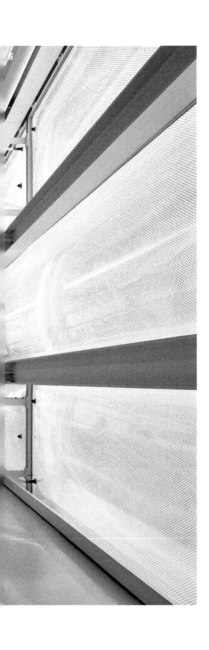

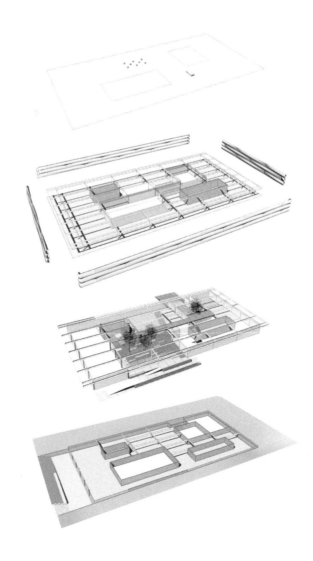

Previous **The ETFE foil is 1% the weight of glass and gives the building a cloud-like appearance.**

The dynamic facade controls incoming solar energy through sophisticated pneumatics.

The building takes on a lantern-like
quality at night.

860–880 Lake Shore Drive

John Ronan

How strange they must have looked when completed in 1951: elegant and mysterious, identical twin towers standing in dialogue at the city's edge, their radically reduced palette of steel, aluminum, and glass more like the cars rushing past on Lake Shore Drive below than the stone buildings nearby. Described in the sales brochure as "a spectacular upsweep of glass and steel,"[1] their facades seem to alternate between transparency and opacity, one face opening up while the other closes down. Each reveals, in a radical breach of protocol, the structural steel frame concealed behind the neighboring stone and brick edifices. The apartment interiors were similarly radical: windows of "thick plate glass ... housed in specially designed aluminum frames"[2] are bisected by the horizon line of Lake Michigan, offering an ever-changing minimalist artwork, one's very own Mark Rothko.

The buildings' architect, Ludwig Mies van der Rohe (1886–1969), the German-born son of a stonemason, had made his name in Europe for his abandonment first of historical styles, then of ornament altogether, in such notable structures as the Barcelona Pavilion (1929). Mies was the director of the renowned Bauhaus when it was effectively shut down by the Nazis in 1933. With opportunities in his homeland dwindling, he fled in 1938 to the United States, where he was invited to run the school of architecture at the Armour Institute (later the Illinois Institute of Technology) in Chicago. Mies's stripped-down aesthetic found a welcome home in the city, the no-nonsense capital of the Midwest.

Commissioned by real estate mogul Herbert Greenwald, the developer-friendly (read: economical) design for 860–880 Lake Shore Drive is the result not of a burst of inspiration but rather of decades of research and experimentation into materials and construction. Here the architect realized his true expression of the steel-and-glass building, with all ornament stripped away until only essential elements remain. As the sales brochure for the buildings states, "The design is so simple, so clean,

1   *860–880 Lake Shore Drive* ([Chicago]: 860 Lake Shore Drive Trust, [ca. 1951]), n.p.
2   *860–880 Lake Shore Drive* (note 1).

so uncluttered by meaningless detail."[3] Germans had a word for this—
Sachlikheit—a certain matter-of-fact quality that implies objectivity.
Mies called it something else: "skin and bones architecture."

For Mies design was the result of a rational and empirical
process, involving the important question of "how," not "what":

> I tried . . . to develop a clear structure. We are just confronted
> with the material. How to use it in the right way is what you
> have to find out. It has nothing to do with the shape. What
> I do—what you call my kind of architecture—we should just
> call it a structural approach. We don't think about the form
> when we start. We think about the right way to use the
> materials. Then we accept the result.[4]

That represented not merely a stylistic alternative but a
radical new approach to building design that even *sounded* different,
for Mies spoke not in the flowery artistic terms of his some of his
contemporaries but with the mathematical objectivity of a scientist.
For him buildings are less artistic creations than objective "solutions" to
the "problem" of building, his conclusions carrying with them the authority
of an essential rightness with which any rational architect would concur.
And so many did. Mies's steel-and-glass solution would be imitated ad
infinitum across the American landscape (including by Mies himself),
though it would never be improved upon. In retrospect the uneven quality
of 860–880's descendants serves to foreground the deceptive simplicity
of Mies's design and expose its real truth: 860–880 Lake Shore Drive is not
an objective "solution" to a building "problem" but a rather subjective and
enigmatic work of art.

3   *860–880 Lake Shore Drive* (note 1).
4   Cited in Moises Puente, *Conversations with Mies van der Rohe* (Princeton, NJ: Princeton Architectural Press, 2008), 58.

This essay was originally published in *Chicago by the Book: 101 Publications That Shaped the City and Its Image,* The University of Chicago Press, 2018.

213

2015

The Spatial Icon
University Conference Center (Invited Competition, 2015)

Can a building be both spatial and iconic? That was the question
we explored when our firm and three others were invited to participate
in a competition for a conference center at the University of Chicago.
The university was nearing the end of a long building spree, during
which numerous iconic buildings by famous architects were added
to the campus, which was starting to look like a butterfly collection.
These buildings felt to me somewhat placeless and portable, as if they
could be picked up and plopped down on any other campus. In my
opinion and that of many others, none of the new additions could be
classified as the best work of any of the hired "starchitects," but this did
not deter the university from their chosen course. The university made
this clear to us and the other three competing firms, doubling down
and stating explicitly in the brief that they desired a "signature" building,
using the term "iconic" more than once to describe the desired outcome.

The history of architecture at the University of Chicago has, in some
ways, mirrored the trajectory of the architecture profession. The traditional campus was space dominant/building recessive: the buildings
were similar and the emphasis was on the spaces between them.
In the 1950s, object-like buildings around framed courtyards appeared:
for example, Eero Saarinen's law school. In the 1970s, courtyards
disappeared and new buildings, such as SOM's Regenstein Library,
were more object-like and had only residual space around them.
In the 1990s and 2000s, another style took hold, that of self-referential
object buildings surrounded by lawn.

The university's stated preference that the conference center be another
signature or iconic building presented a dilemma for me. My work
is known more for its experiential aspects and for exploring spatial
layering and materiality, and I had always resisted the trend toward
one-liner, photogenic, "money shot" architecture. However, I did not
want to disappoint the university, which had selected us, and I wanted
to win the competition. I began to question if a more spatially layered
architecture was indeed incompatible with the iconic, and that perhaps
we could use this opportunity to explore that question. Our design
was an attempt to reclaim the spatial qualities of the historical campus
while delivering the iconicity that the university championed.

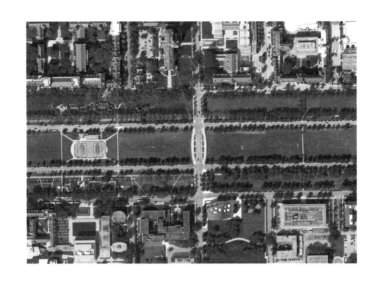

In our proposal, a subtle shift in the fronting street is registered in the angular facade of the conference center, which torques the building's volume and orients it towards the landmark Rockefeller Chapel. Emerging from a bosque, the building rises up in front of you like a high cliff of angular red stone. Its irregular carved openings reflect the variety of meeting spaces inside. A layered spatial sequence begins at the property edge with steps that lead up to a porch and into the building through a covered, wood-ceilinged arcade. The sequence references the spatial typology of the historical campus and roots the design in place.

Once inside, the visitor enters a tall, wood-ceilinged "living room" with a sunken lounge and fireplace. Meeting rooms of various shapes and sizes on the floors above offer framed views of campus, and at the roof level a large terrace backed by an ivy-covered wall offers dramatic views of the city. I felt that providing this view was important because what many conference-goers see of the city is limited to glimpses through their taxicab windows while riding to and from the event. The numerous terraces scattered across the exterior were planted with ivy, which, over time, would creep out over the façade and connect the new building with its campus predecessors, becoming part of the ensemble.

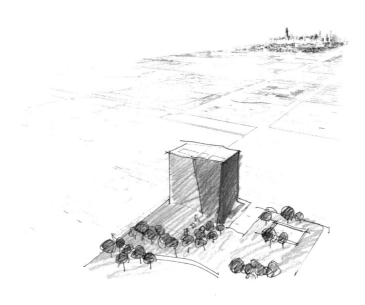

The building's angular façade registers
a subtle shift in the fronting street.

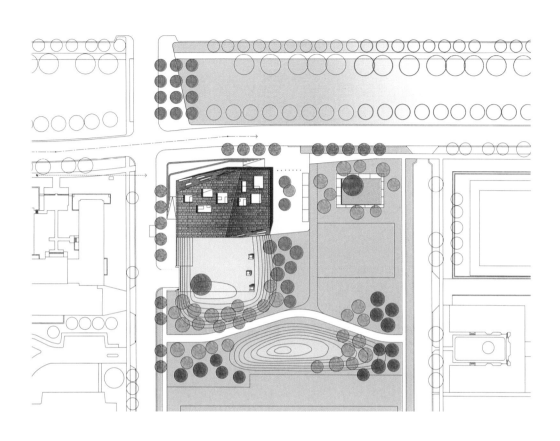

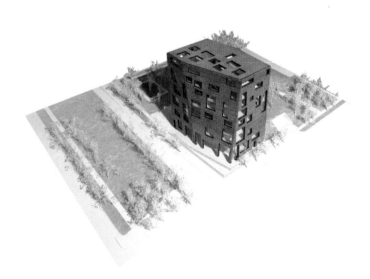

219

Ivy planted in the terraces would grow across the façade over time, connecting the building to its campus predecessors.

A raised porch and wood-ceilinged arcade creates a layered entry sequence into the building, referencing existing campus spatial typologies.

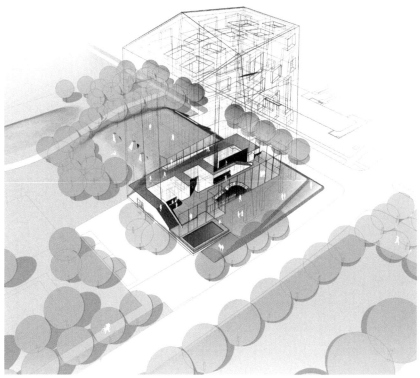

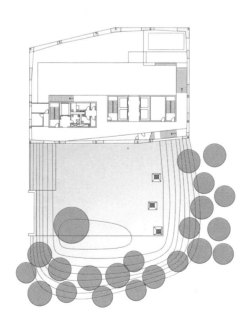

A lounge on the mezzanine level leads
outside to a grassy courtyard encircled
with trees.

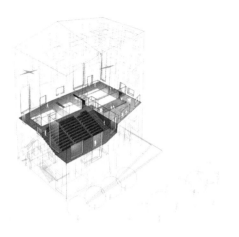

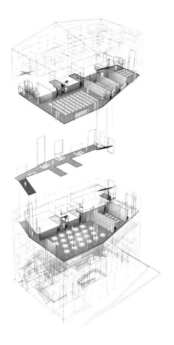

Meeting rooms in varying sizes on the
floors above offer framed views of campus.
An ivy-covered terrace at roof level provides
a dramatic urban panorama.

2016

Hope and Optimism
The Obama Presidential Center (Invited Competition, 2016)

In early 2016, our firm received a call informing us that we were one of the five finalists selected to design the Obama Presidential Center, a combined presidential library and museum with community-based programming. Given that the Obama Foundation had not yet decided between the two Chicago sites in consideration—one in Jackson Park and the other in Washington Park—all the finalists were asked to do a scheme for each park.

The two sites were quite different. Washington Park is in a poverty-stricken area of the city plagued by drugs and gangs and badly in need of investment. To put the presidential center in this location would be a bold break with presidential library precedent. Jackson Park, on Lake Michigan, is a large civic open space already home to one of Chicago's most celebrated institutions, the Museum of Science and Industry; placing the center there presented an opportunity to extend the legacy of Chicago's lakefront museums southward.

The open space of the Jackson Park site (which was ultimately chosen) clearly called for an object building that I hoped would capture the hope and optimism of the Obama presidency. Our proposed building would be in dialogue with the park's vast lakefront landscape, could be seen from multiple vantage points, and offer views in all directions. To achieve this, we planned to reattach to the park a parcel of land that had been split off by a street.

The site is flanked by Hyde Park Academy and the aforementioned Museum of Science and Industry, two very large blocky structures designed in the classical language—both of which are significantly greater in mass than the new presidential center would be. For this reason, I felt not only that the presidential center required a formal identity distinct from these blocky neighbors but also that we needed to enhance the its perceived mass if it were going to hold its own against them. To this end, we lifted the building off the ground and placed it on a seemingly random array of columns and hollowed out its center, creating an elliptical void. These strategies increased the building's perceived height and mass. The void slopes to the east, serving as a natural amphitheater, and when the doors of the auditorium are open,

231

The grand civic landscape of Jackson Park
suggested an object building.

it becomes an indoor/outdoor performance space, with the lagoon as its backdrop. The open, grassy void puts people at the project's center, symbolizing the collective action to which the Obamas have dedicated their lives.

Visitors enter the building from the north or south. The large glass-enclosed main lobby leads to the main dining/event space and the outdoor dining terrace beyond, with its view of the lagoon and the Science and Industry Museum. Stairs leading down from the lobby access the auditorium at water level.

An ornamental stair at the south end of the lobby leads to the museum level, where the transparent shell allows visitors circulating through the exhibitions to gaze out over the surrounding neighborhood and parkland before being returned to the lobby. They can also look across the inner ring to the spaces dedicated to community programs, making a connection between the museum and the Obama Foundation's ongoing activism. The upper floors house the document archive and foundation offices and offer panoramic views of Lake Michigan and, by implication, the world beyond.

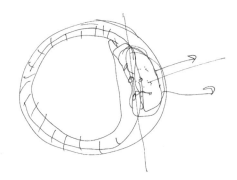

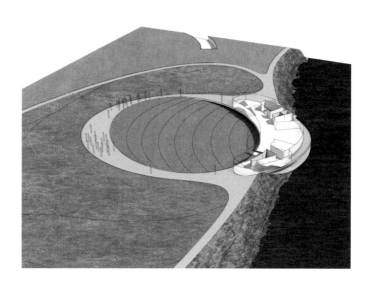

A sloping grass amphitheater places the public at the project's center.

235

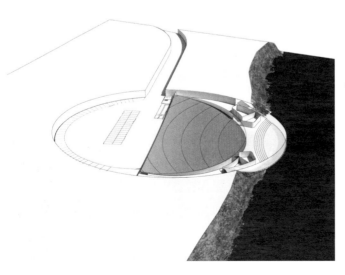

A water-level auditorium offers views of the adjacent landscape and nearby landmark museum.

237

The museum-goers path is a continuous circuit offering views in all directions.

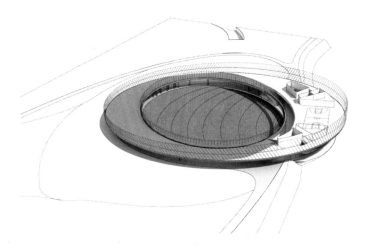

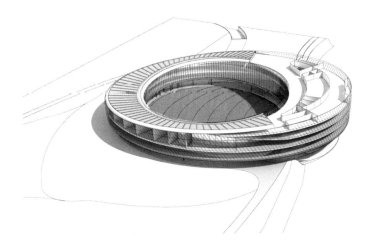

On the lagoon's island we proposed an
urban campground for young people
visiting the site.

241

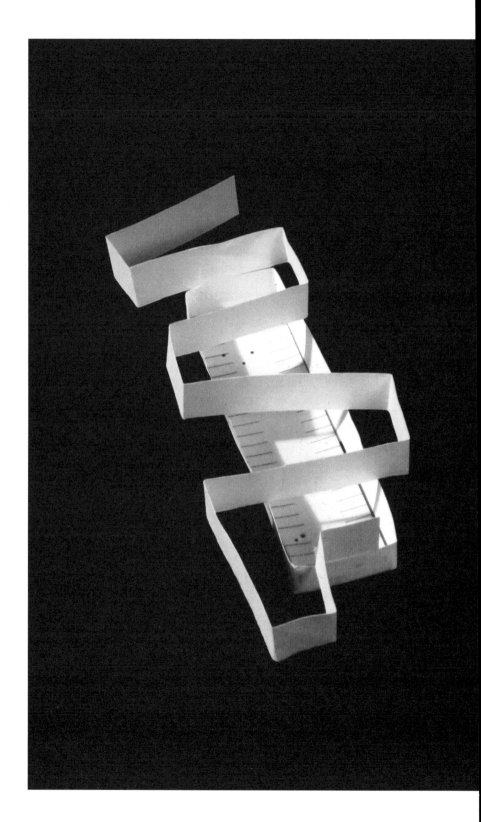

2017

Wallflower
The University of Cincinnati Alumni Center (2017)

Over the years, the University of Cincinnati had invited a who's who
of prominent architects to write their signatures on the campus.
Now the university grounds resembled a crowded room of raucous
partygoers in a Jacques Tati film, avoiding dialogue but having a great
time all the same. We had been invited to add an alumni center to this
ensemble. It was to be located on the southern edge of campus
and would serve as both a welcoming center and a campus gateway.
The university was running out of space on its hilly and cramped
campus, and the site, an oddly shaped and steeply sloping leftover,
also had to accommodate a generously sized parking lot.

Our design would act as a kind of filter; it would allow faculty and
students to pass through but would invite alumni to linger and
reminisce and, perhaps, be enticed to donate to their alma mater.
The building *parti* was that of a continuously snaking wall that both
accommodates program and frames views of campus. Visitors move
crosswise through the walls in a slowly unfolding spatial sequence
of gallery-like museum spaces in which artifacts of university history
are displayed along the way to meeting rooms of various sizes.
Throughout this path, outside views alternate between campus and
city to connect alumni with memories of their university years.

Structurally, the two-story zig-zagging wall acts like a beam spanning
between concrete walls embedded into the hillside which frame the
covered parking below.

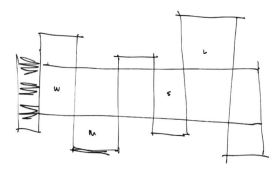

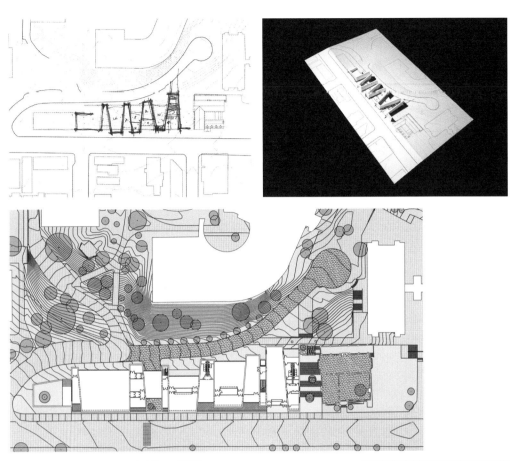

Cladding the wall with a local limestone rooted the building in place. We located the gateway for faculty and students—a thirty-foot grand stair that descends to the main campus—between the alumni center and an adjacent historically significant YMCA building. Our introverted alumni center stands pressed up against the edge of campus like a wallflower surveying the crowd of rollicking buildings below, each vying to be the center of attention. Our building stands quietly observing the party, but resists joining it.

The building *parti* is a continuously snaking wall that accommodates program and frames views of campus.

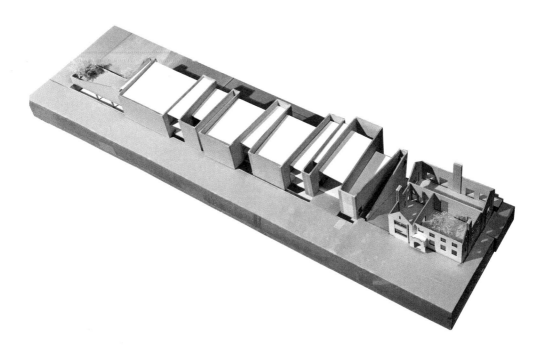

The two-story, stone-clad walls act like structural beams spanning between the concrete walls of the parking level below, embedded into the campus hillside.

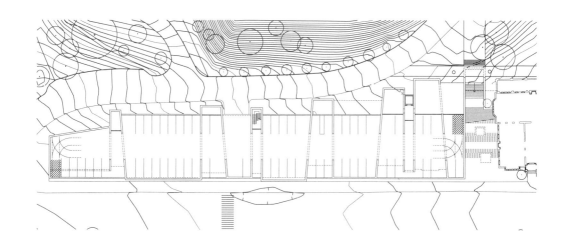

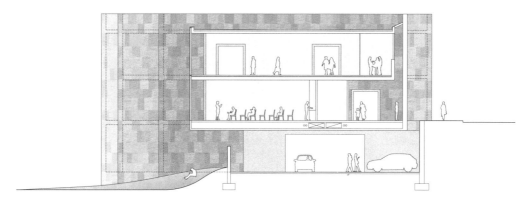

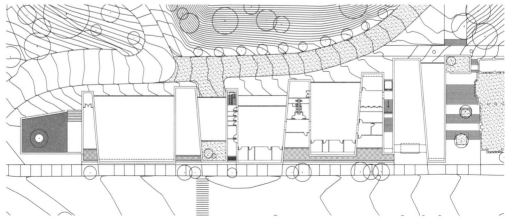

248

Visitors travel through the walls in a slowly unfolding spatial sequence of gallery-like museum spaces.

Reflections on the work of John Ronan

Carlos Jimenez

John Ronan, born and raised in Grand Rapids Michigan, is the quintessential Chicago architect, inspired and empowered by working in a city with such formidable lineage. Ronan's commitment to his adoptive city affirms the faith that architects bring to this demanding yet ever welcoming metropolis. He maintains that the object of architecture is not to "razzle dazzle" an anxious present, or align itself with the market, but rather to project and build the city. Examining Ronan's body of work, one understands how critical his commitment to Chicago is, a charge that begins with the strategic selection of a material, or by optimizing the constraints of a building's budget, or by taking a measure of the pulse of the city's-built heritage. Lately John Ronan and his associates have participated in a series of invited competitions from Dublin to Moscow. Yet his office remains invested in such home-based projects as the Headquarters of the Chicago Park District and the Frank Lloyd Wright Trust Visitor Center. I would like to highlight four recently built works by this indefatigable architect that display his resolve and sensibilities as he now launches his practice into its third decade.

The Poetry Foundation, completed in 2011, is a discreet building at the corner of West Superior and North Dearborn streets. During the day the building's perimeter façade, a veil of perforated oxidized zinc, barely hints at its luminous interior. Demure in the bustle of the city, the Poetry Foundation is a sanctuary where the works of poets exude an aura of wonder in layered spatial reciprocity. Upon entering the building's corner threshold, one is beckoned by a garden of zigzagging trees, a virtual decompression chamber. The sounds of the city slowly recede as a soothing stillness transfigures the entire space. Seeing, hearing, arriving, perusing, lingering, touching, pausing, meandering - all actions akin to reading poetry - find their counterpart in each carefully chosen material. The Poetry Foundation is a tactile and visual narrative in which sandblasted concrete planks, moss and gravel inlets, aluminum fins, clear glass planes, and Baltic birch plywood, spell out lyrical associations, bridging or echoing spatial pauses, mirroring correspondences. Exterior and interior spaces become one multilayered, circular event that allows the visitor to recall specific passages, as if collecting epigrams from what becomes an indelible sensual experience. Each visit will be different, even after your second, third or however many readings thereafter.

At the Illinois Institute of Technology (IIT), Ludwig Mies van der Rohe's buildings line up as orderly, hermetic figures of an extended family whose modern features give the campus its formal and material palette. Mies's buildings, interspersed with green spaces and acacia trees, remain unperturbed in their partial opacity and rational demeanor. Such recent additions to the campus as OMA's McCormick Center (2003) attempt to shake up the rigorous layout by Mies. Yet the provocation introduced by the McCormick Center faded quickly. Ronan's *IIT Innovation Center (2019),* the most recent addition to the campus, introduces a perceptive counterpoint to Mies's rigorous layout. Ronan does not trivialize or slash the Miesian box, or for that matter dismisses its modular pedigree. Rather he opens it up in incandescent and inviting ways. Ronan accepts as a given the 12 x 24-foot grid system and like a master surgeon begins to make strategic cuts and openings to reveal a spatial and urban complexity absent from the Miesian language. The introduction of vertical courtyards and a column-less arcade does wonders for the campus, offering students outdoor spaces to sit, study, gather or rest. The primary materials used for the building's exterior - large insulated glass panels at the ground floor, capped by ETFE air-supported cushions that not only float but breathe in pneumatic intervals – enhance the sensation of buoyancy. At times, particularly in the early evening, the building appears like an improbable, magical act. The placid composure of its envelope gives way upon entering to a dynamic and flexible interior, where the spirit of innovation courses through open and subdivided rooms alike. Sectional shifts occur in strategic areas, attenuating the dominant horizontly of the floor plates.

The Independence Library and Apartments (2019) is a work of urban ingenuity and civic pride, grafting a hybrid type to an area of historic and contemporary buildings, and a few houses that date back to the late nineteenth century. Located in the Irwin Park district on Chicago's

Northwest side, the 60,000 square foot building replaces a neighborhood library that burned, while adding 44 affordable apartment units for senior citizens, parking, a communal garden and other amenities. What impresses one is the confidence with which two building types, with contrasting programmatic and exterior conditions have been merged. The library, an uncompromising block of dark gray toned glass and pre-cast concrete panels, becomes a sober yet translucent plinth as it faces the main street, especially at night when its two-level interior glows like a panoramic lantern. Containing the library's staff, reading and shelving requirements in a double-height public room, this plinth is an ideal foreground and base for stacking the apartments above. Though stepping back from the busy street to increase privacy, the apartments are far from shy as each unit claims individuality across the façade. Animated by a syncopated grid of colorful balcony and window openings, the housing block is infused with an infectious vitality. Its exterior also hints at the care given to the interiors, captured in the playful color rotations at each apartment's entry door and mat. The building is constructed with simple, modest materials that in their attentive detailing and application enrich the complex with dignity, one not frequently given to affordable housing enterprises.

151 North Franklin is Ronan's first venture in the highly competitive speculative office market. The 151 North Franklin building is sited at the epicenter of Chicago's Loop financial district. The thirty-six-story office tower is invested with an unexpected set of luxuries that elevate the basic office tower formula. As in Ronan's other works, we encounter another variation of what he refers to as "outdoor rooms", this time an open, corner plaza commensurate in proportion with the tower above. Carved out of the building's base, the four-story "outdoor room" is a meticulously detailed plaza-lobby, inviting tenants, visitors, and pedestrians to an uplifting urban volume. The plaza becomes a platform, a vantage point from which to survey the marvelous enfilade of neighboring buildings or the park across the street. This unanticipated gesture to the connectivity and flow of the Loop is a prelude to the generous lobby, which leads to the elevator core and to a more intimate courtyard on the second level. The lobby unfolds in a musical pattern of jet mist granite panels finished in three distinct textures: sandblasted, flamed and honed. The success of this public space springs not only from the vibrancy generated by the granite panels, but from the sculpted interior's play of scales, at times intimate, at times expansive. Ronan's desire to dissolve the primacy of the single, aloof object building is particularly admirable at a time when most office towers are monuments of self-referential gestures, oblivious of the life of the street.

   At the beginning of my text, I alluded to John Ronan as the consummate Chicago architect, one at ease and conversant with architecture's local and universal bearings. The precision, intelligence and vision that distinguishes his buildings suffuse his built and unbuilt works. These are singular works that enrich and expand their contexts, yet also transcend their specific circumstances, conferring vital lessons for the discipline of architecture at large. Ronan sees architecture as an ethical, transformative endeavor committed to the larger construction of the city. Architecture is not a pageant of instantaneity for the whims of the market or a stage for the vanities of architects. Architecture is a site where optimism prevails, not only in the eloquence of its details, its materiality, its forms, its social contract, but also in its understanding of time as a radical construction. It is always reassuring to find architects who build with time in mind, in which the reality and enigma of all created things reside. Rainer Maria Rilke in one of his Letters to a Young Poet reminds us that *"A work of art is good when it is necessary, when it comes from a need."* In the illusory distractions and endless wants that our consumerist culture thrives on, that Rilkean axiom is more essential than ever.

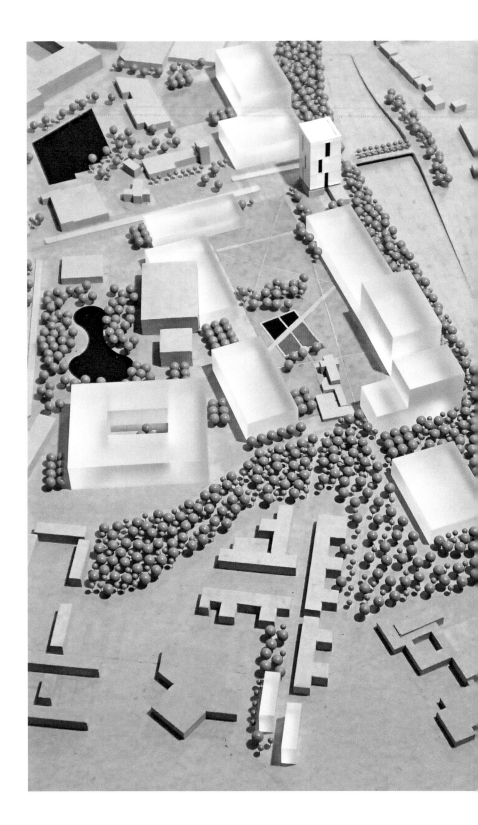

2018

That Lost Feeling
University College Dublin Future Campus
and the Centre for Creative Design (Invited Competition, 2018)

The thing I remember most about the campus buildings were the colored stripes painted on the floor. These are a warning that you are entering a labyrinthine environment, and you're likely to get lost if you don't keep your eye on the colored line guiding you to your destination. This wayfinding trope typically points to some failure in the building design, and I was indeed feeling lost in UCD's maze-like buildings as I toured the campus along with three other architects selected to participate in a design competition to create a new campus master plan and a landmark gateway building, the Centre for Creative Design.

I immediately recognized that our design objective should be to bring much-needed clarity to the original campus plan, which consisted of a systemic framework of crisscrossing linear gray buildings rendered in brutalist concrete. The structures had strong character—if you like that kind of thing—but the campus did not. It seemed as if the planners had focused all their attention on the architecture of the buildings but overlooked the interstitial space, and the resulting campus could boast no memorable outdoor places.

Our Entrance Precinct Master Plan proposed a more pedestrian-friendly campus punctuated by bold and memorable outdoor spaces. Our strategy was premised on controlling the voids between buildings rather than dictating the form or aesthetics of the structures themselves. In our plan, cars are restricted to the perimeter of the pedestrian campus core, and new buildings frame views of bold campus green spaces and the historic estate houses that give the campus its unique sense of place. Given the college's trajectory toward ever larger buildings, the proposed green spaces would be scaled accordingly.

Our proposal transforms the existing "back door" vehicular entry to campus into a "front door" by creating a grand pedestrian boulevard anchored by the new Centre for Creative Design building, which stands like a sentinel marking the main entry to the college for the vast majority of people who arrive at this commuter campus from central Dublin by bus or car. The new building straddles three spatial conditions: entry plaza, perimeter woodland, and campus green.

The Centre for Creative Design building stands like a sentinel marking the main point to campus.

We envisioned the Centre for Creative Design as a monument to innovation. A stark, white monolith, square in plan, which can be seen from great distances, it stands out from its neighbors yet is at home among the campus's neutral-colored structures. Accessible from all sides at grade, its interior spatial narrative unfolds slowly. Wide stairways lead from public spaces on the ground floor to community spaces on the second; upper floors house studios, labs, and collaboration spaces. The pin-wheeling arrangement of the building's plan supports interdisciplinary collaboration—architecture studios and engineering labs share the same floor, and transition zones are places of creative collision. Three-story winter garden lounges interspersed throughout the structure provide year-round connection with nature and act like chimneys to create a stack effect, driving the natural ventilation strategy.

We came in runner-up—the most frustrating possible outcome—to a building that was outrageous formally and a candidate for wayfinding lines painted on the floor. I had always prided myself on being able to render complex design problems in clear, simple terms, but the jury did not buy what I was selling. They awarded us a special commendation "for a master plan of great clarity that was beautifully thought through and a Centre for Creative Design that had gravitas and a gentle, rational strength," which was some consolation, but I realized something important that day. Sometimes people like being lost.

The Centre for Creative Design building
is a stark white monolith which stands out
from its neighbors yet is at home among
the campus' neutral-colored structures.

261

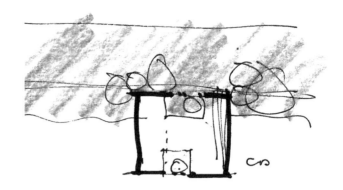

The new building straddles the boundary
between the campus green and
the existing woodland that encircles
the campus.

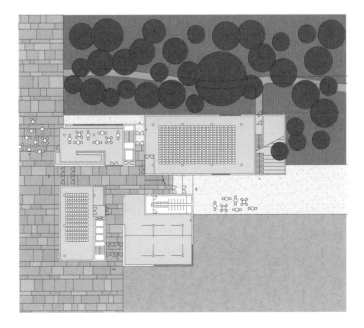

Multi-story winter gardens are interspersed throughout the structure to aid in natural ventilation and provide a year-round connection with nature.

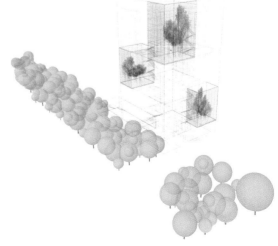

Architecture and engineering studios share the same floor in a pin-wheeling arrangement designed to promote interdisciplinary collaboration.

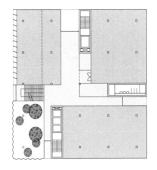
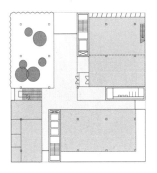
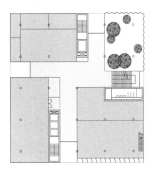

267

2018

A Reclaiming
Lemont Quarries Adventure Park (2018)

The Illinois and Michigan (I & M) Canal, completed in 1848, connected
the Great Lakes to the Mississippi River and from there to the Gulf
of Mexico. When the canal diggers got to Lemont, Illinois, they hit the
yellow, dolomitic limestone that came to be known as Lemont Stone,
a material that was extensively quarried and featured in many of
Chicago's famous buildings. Starting at the turn of twentieth century,
the I & M canal was replaced by larger waterways, and the Lemont
stone industry went into decline. The quarries, now long abandoned
and filled with water, were about to have a second act.

My client, a group of entrepreneurs who made their money in the tech
industry, were reimagining the quarries and the land around them as
a proving ground for testing the limits of physical and mental endurance.
They were counting on people rethinking their life/work balance
as society transitioned from the Industrial Age to the Information Age,
spending less time at the office and more time engaging in activities
designed to bring them personal growth. The quarry site would
be reclaimed as an indoor and outdoor recreational venue, for which
we would design the master plan and a multi-building "base camp"
for indoor climbing, co-working, dining, and events.

Our design was informed by the site's industrial heritage—elemental
and direct, employing rusted steel and board-formed concrete to honor
the hard-working past and to reclaim the atmosphere of an abandoned
quarrying operation. Dolomitic limestone from the site—in the form
of blocks, boulders, dressed stone, and gravel—would comprise the
base camp's walking surfaces to foreground the material and reference
the site's rich physical history.

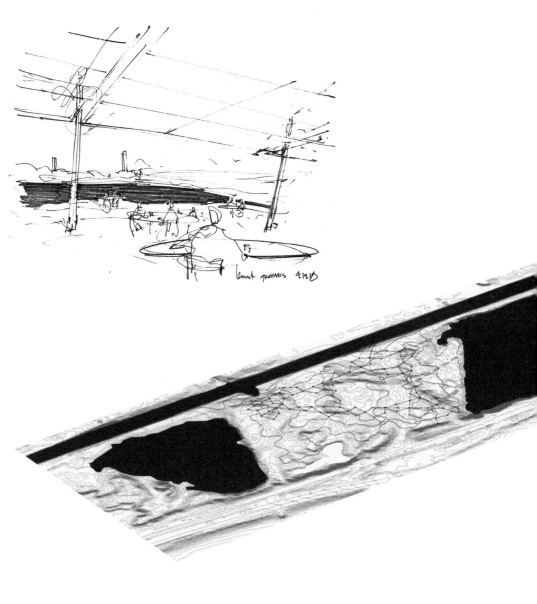

The multi-building base camp draws
on the site's industrial past in its form
and materiality.

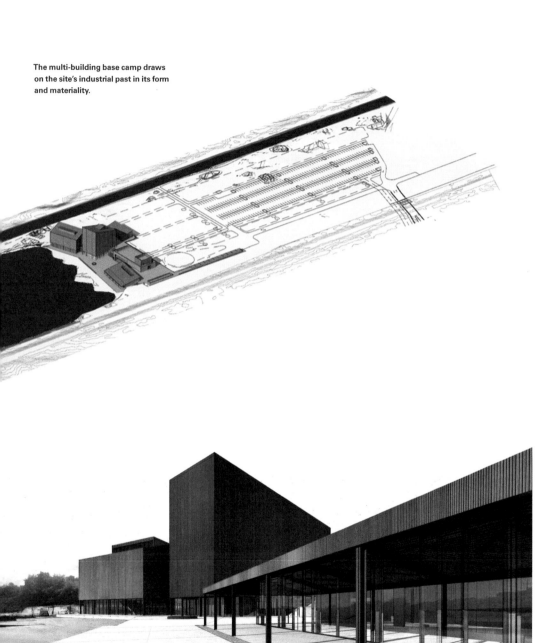

The design of the base camp buildings
is elemental and direct, suggesting an
abandoned quarrying operation.

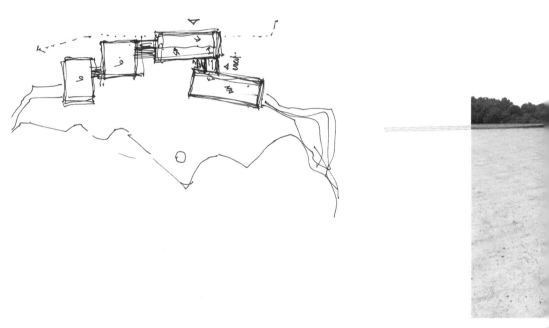

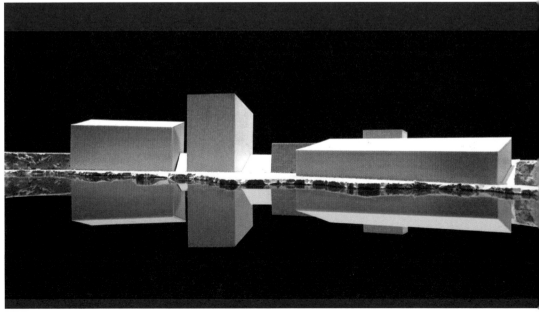

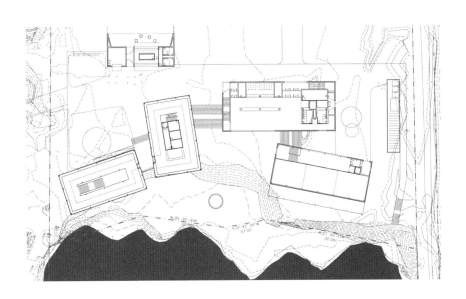

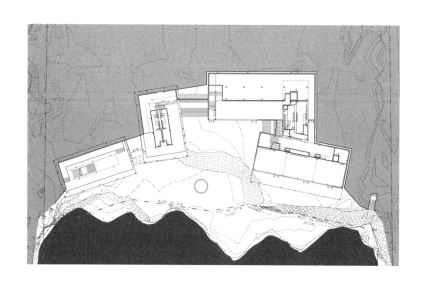

274

The event space overlooks the water which
now fills the abandoned quarry.

Shed-like volumes for climbing straddle
the partially-excavated rock.

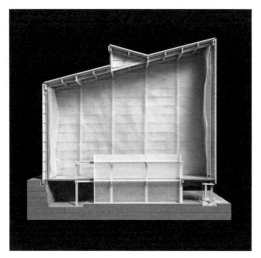

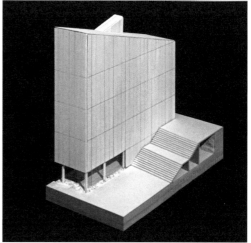

2019

Cross-Fertilization
Independence Library and Apartments (2017–19)

Chicago's reputation in the area of social housing is infamous and well earned. After World War II, large swaths of the city's urban fabric in predominantly African-American neighborhoods were cleared for high-rise housing projects, in the name of "urban renewal." Chicago's version of urban renewal meant identical apartments inside identical buildings stretching for miles on Chicago's south and west sides. Among these modernist monuments to expediency were the Robert Taylor Homes, a seemingly-endless inventory of red brick apartment buildings bordering the the Dan Ryan Expressway, and Stateway Gardens, a conjoined expanse of yellow brick just to their north that extended for miles and presumably marking the point where they ran out of red brick. How ironic that "Home" and "Garden" so often found their way into the names of these barren places, as if in an attempt to conceal the sad truth that they were neither. The people who lived there called them "The Projects." They knew them for what they were—warehouses for the poor.

When the housing projects first opened, they were desirable places to live, but a series of disastrous policy decisions—some well-intentioned and some not—by the Chicago Housing Authority soon made their design failures apparent. When the CHA reset rents as a percentage of income rather than flat rates, higher-income tenants migrated out, and their absence caused a revenue shortfall that was taken out of the maintenance budget. The cheaply-constructed buildings quickly fell into disrepair when maintenance was neglected. The few number of entry and exit points in each tower made them easily controlled by gangs, who eventually took control. By the 1990s, the living conditions in these towers had become so unsafe and unhealthy that the federal government mandated demolition if Chicago was to receive any future federal funds for public housing. So down they came. The problematic social conditions incubated in this architectural experiment did not disappear with the towers, however; it moved into the adjoining neighborhoods, where the city now built smaller scale "scattered site" affordable housing. That history provides the context for our first foray into affordable housing. We had won a competition for a 44-unit affordable-housing project for seniors combined with a public library branch in a North Side neighborhood where the previous branch had recently burned down. The idea to combine the two typologies came

from Mayor Rahm Emmanuel and was financed through an innovative model involving federal low-income housing tax credits.

By that time of the competition, we already had gained something of a reputation for designing hybrid buildings. Our proposal for the Perth Amboy High School in 2003 was quickly followed by a Public Building Commission of Chicago offer to design a prototype high school. Applying our research from Perth Amboy, we proposed that the school's library double as a branch library for the community after school hours, and four such high schools based on our Urban Model High School Prototype had been built. The Independence Library and Apartments was a chance to go further into combining programmatically divergent typologies, in this case by crossbreeding the library with housing.

I wanted the building to be more than the sum of its parts. The site was very compact and the library would need to be multi-story to accommodate the required on-site parking, so we proposed an outdoor garden above the parking at the library's second floor. This created a park-like amenity for library users and tenants where the two constituencies could intermingle. Thus, the design's parti is comprised of a two-story library element, slid forward to the street-facing property line to foreground its public nature, and a four-story residential block, set back from the street to create an entry courtyard for both buildings. The ground floor of the bi-level library houses the children's section and a large multipurpose room for community gatherings and events. When the library is closed, this room can be entered directly from the street. The second floor is dedicated to adults and to teens. We hired a local street artist to paint a mural of Chicago authors in the teen room.

The recessed residential block creates an entry court.

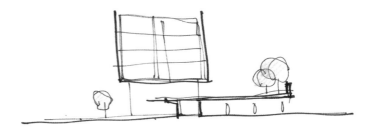

The façade departs from the monotonous
repetition which characterizes Chicago's
past efforts in social housing.

284

Although the budget was small, I wanted of the library to recall the grand reading rooms of the past. Chicago had been building uninspiring one-story, cookie-cutter libraries until recently and I wanted to reclaim the dignity that civic libraries once had. The main, 40-feet high library space has natural light coming in on three sides, and a monumental bleacher/stair connects the two levels and provides a place for community lectures and gatherings. The library's grey poured-in-place concrete structure provides a neutral backdrop for colorful walls and furniture, which subdivides the large loft-like space into smaller room-like areas and reference the building's colored apartment balconies above.

In an effort to transcend the brutal pragmatism that had previously characterized Chicago's social housing, all apartments feature brightly-colored balconies recessed into the façade in a staggered pattern to emphasize the individual amidst the collective, and enabling residents to identify their apartment from the street. I wanted to create something that felt like a "home" rather than "housing." Hallway apartment doors are color coordinated to match the unit's balcony color; the brightly-colored doors animate the hallway and help seniors easily locate their unit.

The design period was compressed into eight months to fast-track a schedule timed to the election cycle. It included a robust community engagement process involving alderman from four wards, four city agencies, and a steering committee comprised of representatives of nine community groups. The construction had to be completed in twelve months and, to complicate matters further, the library needed to open ahead of the apartments and prior to the election.

This compressed delivery schedule informed the design. We built the library in concrete and utilized a steel structure for the apartment building; this allowed construction trades to continue work inside the library while the steel frame was still being erected above it. To enclose the building quickly, so that construction could continue inside during the winter months, we employed weathertight insulated aluminum panels. A rainscreen cladding was added the following spring. The library's ground-and-polished precast concrete panels were erected in a single day.

A landscaped terrace at the second level over the parking lot creates a park-like amenity space for both tenants and library-goers.

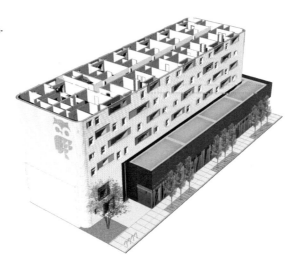

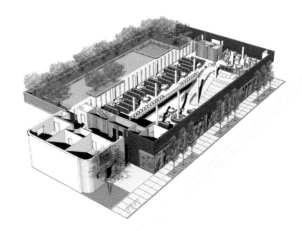

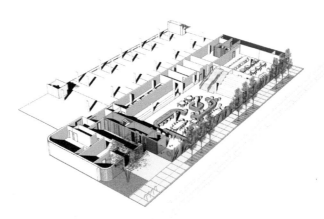

As the building neared completion, negotiations ensued between the developer and library over responsibility for security at the second floor public garden space, intended to be a "social condenser" where library users and tenants would mingle which brought to mind the difficult lesson from Chicago's past—that design and policy must work hand-in-hand to be effective. Eventually a compromise was reached that allowed library patrons and residents to use the park together and help realize the innovative model's promise of community building.

I felt the project aspirations of restoring dignity to the architecture of the public realm had been realized, but more importantly we had fulfilled an important potential—to positively impact the way Chicagoans think about affordable housing in their neighborhood and begin to right old wrongs. The project conveyed the message that design should not be used to isolate and categorize people by wealth or circumstance but to integrate everyone into the larger community, and that having housing is not the same as having a home.

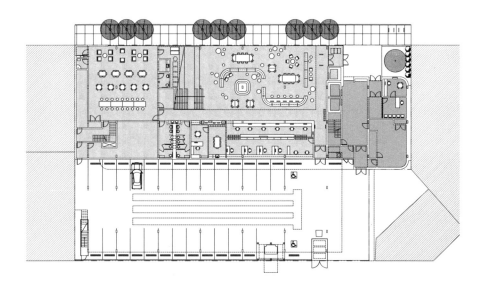

292

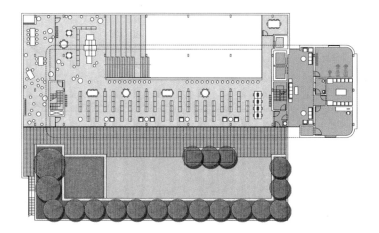

Clerestory glazing allows daylight to enter
the library on three sides.

A local street artist was hired to paint
a mural of renowned Chicago authors
in the teen space.

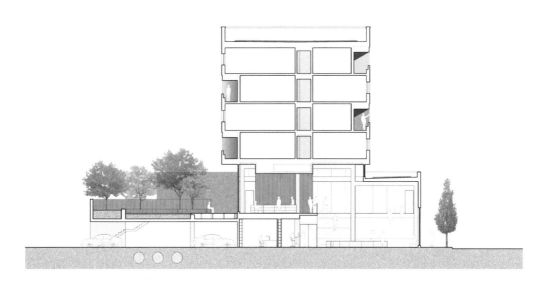

Apartment entrances are color-coordinated with the unit balconies to animate the corridors and aid in navigation.

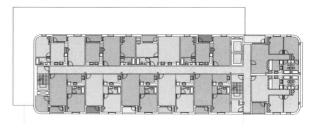

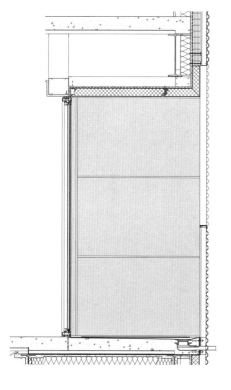

The library is clad in ground-and-polished precast concrete panels to distinguish it from the residential block.

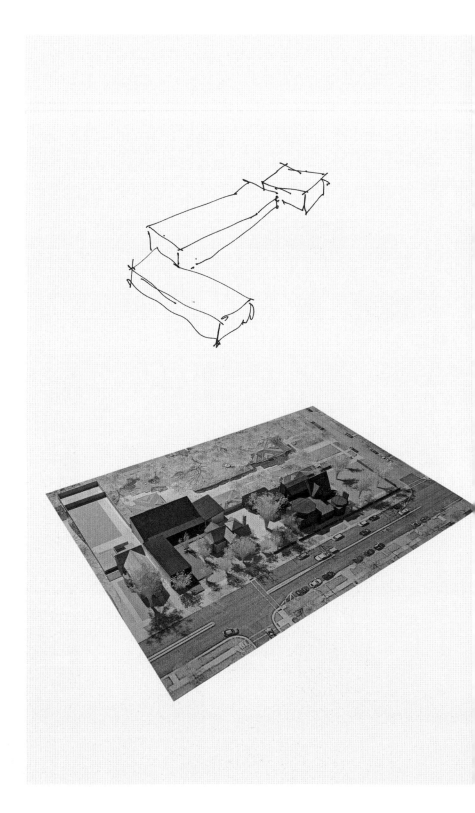

2022

A Cultural Inheritance

Frank Lloyd Wright Home and Studio Museum Learning Center
(2018–22)

Year after year, and from all over the world, thousands come to the little town outside Chicago. The Village of Oak Park is something like a Lourdes for design mavens, who make the pilgrimage to visit the work of the twentieth century's greatest American architect, Frank Lloyd Wright. The town that Ernest Hemingway dismissed as a place of "wide streets and narrow minds" is, in fact, a treasure trove of *Wrightiana*, home to many of the most renowned homes from the early, Prairie style, stage of his career, which is arguably when he made his greatest contribution to architecture. That so many make this journey is a testament both to the architect's genius and to his staying power and is a reminder of the obligations of stewardship that a cultural inheritance imposes. This stewardship is the responsibility of the Frank Lloyd Trust, whose mission is to preserve, and to educate the public about, Wright's work. It is rare for an architect's legacy to be protected in this way. The Trust owns and operates Wright's Home and Studio in Oak Park, which he built for himself next to a house for his mother, Anna, and where he lived until 1909. Here, visitors can tour the master's home and see the studio where so many important works originated. Tours of other Wright houses in the neighborhood and of nearby Unity Temple originate from this site. We won an invited competition by the Frank Lloyd Wright Trust to design a museum, a learning center, and a space to accommodate tour groups, educational programs, and public events. Our challenge was akin to writing the foreword to classic novel that would frame and interpret it for a contemporary audience.

The site is densely built — over time, Wright had made several additions to his house and his mother's— and there was little room left for a new structure. The L-shaped, one-story pavilion brackets one end of the site and is comprised of three interconnected volumes– a reception hall, an event/exhibition space, and a studio for design classes—under a roof of continuously folded oxidized zinc. One of the exterior walls is covered in this material, while the others are glazed. The studio classroom and event hall are enclosed in clear glass and the back-of-house spaces in sandblasted mirrored glass. Slate platforms lead from the sidewalk to the front door of the museum and serve as gathering areas for tour

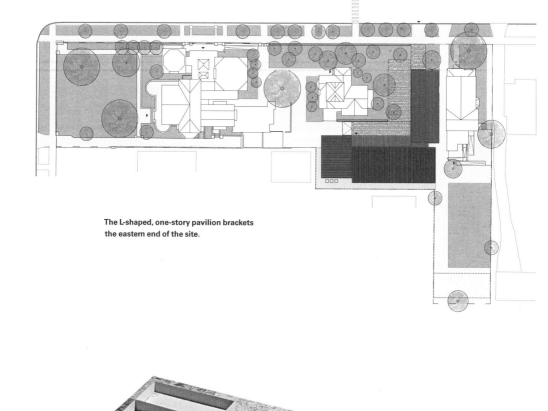

The L-shaped, one-story pavilion brackets
the eastern end of the site.

groups and to accommodate spillover from events. On the interior, flooring of stone, wood, and terrazzo distinguishes the three public spaces, respectively. A support structure of steel bars to which the glazing is affixed is exposed to view before disappearing behind a diaphanous stretch-fabric scrim at the ceiling. Door openings allow free movement between the pavilion interior and outdoor slate terraces, thoughtfully placed into the surface of the historically sensitive site.

The pavilion is neither a slavish homage to Wright's work nor defined in opposition to it. Its role is to provide a dignified structure in which to interpret and celebrate the life and work of a modern master .

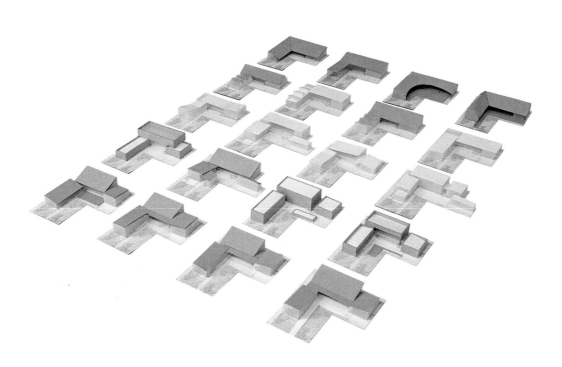

A continuous folding plane of oxidized zinc forms the roof and walls of the pavilion.

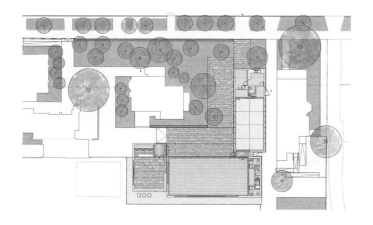

Stone platforms lead to the pavilion
entrance and serve as gathering areas
for tours and events.

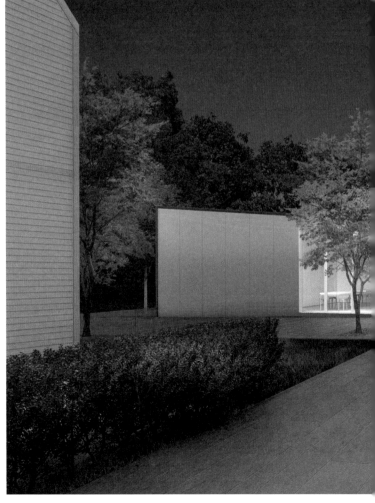

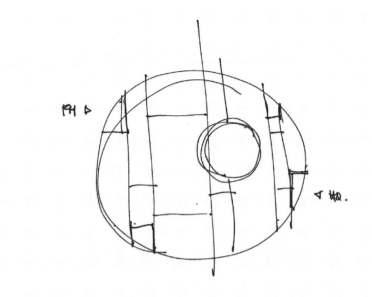

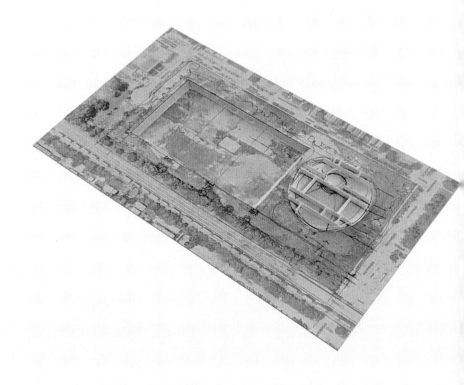

Dignifying Work
Chicago Park District Headquarters (2019–22)

The city, having recently decided to start moving administrative departments out of the downtown districts and into the neighborhoods, commissioned us to design the first of these efforts, a new headquarters for the Chicago Park District. The commission included the headquarters building, along with a field house and seventeen-acre public park, on a formerly industrial site in Chicago's Brighton Park neighborhood

Judging by old photographs, the original 1939 headquarters building, demolished to make way for the expansion of Soldier Field on Chicago's lakefront, had a quiet dignity and looks like it must have been a great place to work. A monumental stair led up to the colonnaded entry porch; I thought the high-ceilinged, wood-paneled boardroom would have inspired elevated discourse; and the landscaped outdoor courtyard for relaxing, socializing, and having lunch under the trees signaled respect for the staff. It was a far cry from the three floors of the nondescript 1969 office tower that at the time was home to the Chicago Park District headquarters. Owing to the building's copper reflective glass windows, the interior of the office was dark, no matter the weather or time of day. The boring sameness of the space made it difficult to navigate; hallways lined with lateral file cabinets separated a sea of cubicles from the characterless and cramped perimeter offices. I got lost upon every visit and even gaining admittance felt like an act of transgression. There was no receptionist; instead, staff were contacted via a wall-mounted landline phone from the hallway, which only added to the prison-like atmosphere. Once inside, the only navigational cues were provided by the personal items people left lying around: the office with a desk stacked with papers three feet high in a gravity-defying act of deferred filing, the cubicle with the coffee maker and toaster oven, the desk with the Christmas ornaments.

Chicago's park system is one of the city's most valuable assets, and I felt its stewards should be entitled to a humane and respectful workplace. I saw the project as an opportunity to reclaim some of the lost dignity of old headquarters building and to reset the relationship between the Park District staff and the community it serves.

The site plan strategy was informed by
Olmsted's Park and Boulevard System
for Chicago.

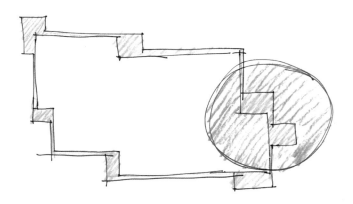

318

We decided to combine the headquarters and field house into one structure bisected by a path that continues around the park, and gave it an iconic circular form befitting an important civic institution. In researching historic Chicago parks, we noticed that their field houses were located not on the street but set back into the middle of the park, which organized the parkland into discrete zones. We decided to adopt this strategy for the combined headquarters/fieldhouse structure, siting it in the midst of the park and using it to organize the surrounding landscape and recreational areas.

To the west of the building, we proposed a Grand Lawn surrounded by trees and, beyond it, playing fields. To the east is a large meadow, with walking paths, which serves as building foreground from the main approach on Western Avenue. To the north is a children's area, with playground and splash pad. We located parking to the south of the building, at the base of a railroad track embankment.

A continuous pathway through the park makes its way around the playing fields and bisects the circular building structure into its two constituent components: headquarters and field house. Once inside the building's precinct, the path widens into a pair of open-air courtyards that serve as outdoor relaxation spaces for staff and bring daylight to the inner reaches of the large building floor plate.

Inside the headquarters, alternating bands of enclosed offices and large, flexible open office areas promote a culture of collaboration and exchange. The walls forming these bands are made of bearing masonry clad in reclaimed Chicago common brick to root it in place. Spanning between the walls is a floor structure of steel bar joists and concrete-filled metal deck topped with terrazzo. The economical structure is enclosed with a unitized curtain wall with integral expanded metal sunshade whose curving geometry echoes the overall building form.

The headquarters and field house were combined in one structure to connect the Park District staff to the community they serve. Open office areas on both levels allow views into the surrounding park, and areas on the second floor for breaks and casual work overlook the field house gym, so staff can watch a basketball game in progress while eating lunch or working on Park District business. Fitness and exercise rooms in the field house are accessible via internal stair to Park District staff, who are provided with a dignified work environment in a public park setting.

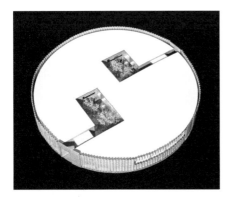

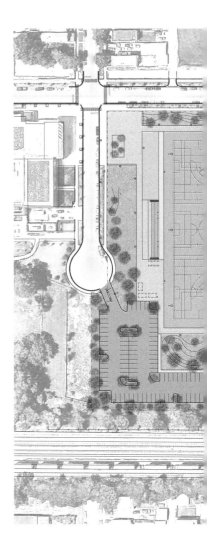

A continuous park pathway passes through
the building, bisecting it into headquarters
and fieldhouse.

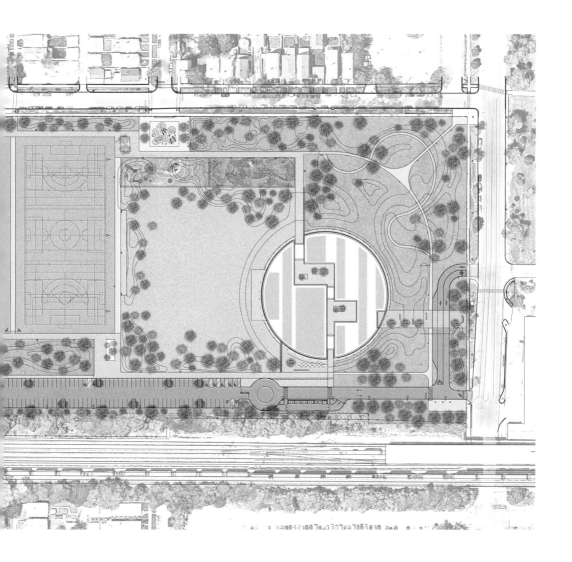

The building in construction (October 2021)

The prak pathway widens into courtyards
as it passes through the building.

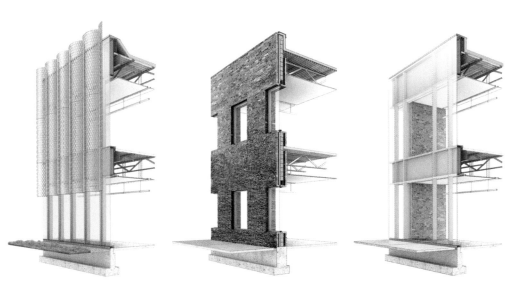

Fieldhouse club rooms have a view of the
adjacent park and playing fields beyond.

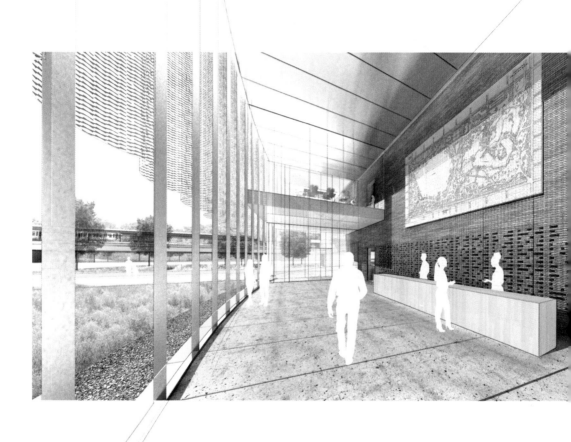

A staff break room has views into
the courtyard and gym below.

The Next Bauhaus

John Ronan

The Bauhaus is the Keith Richards of design schools: influential, legendary and stubbornly refusing to die. The fanfare occasioned by its 100th anniversary is largely deserved—it's still the gold standard among design schools—but the fact that it was in existence only for fourteen years raises the obvious question, "Why are we still talking about the Bauhaus?" and a more elusive one, "Why has no design school superseded its influence in the intervening century?"

If we're talking about the school, rather than the style, we need to acknowledge that there is no such thing as the Bauhaus. The school went through several manifestations during its short existence, so it is only one thing in the same way a caterpillar and a butterfly are one thing: the school that Walter Gropius started in 1919 bears little resemblance to the school Mies would disband in 1933. Gropius' utopian vision of uniting all the arts under one roof where they could cross-fertilize was the central idea behind its founding, reminiscent of composer Richard Wagner's earlier efforts to unify all arts via opera into "the total work of art." This Germanic predilection for overarching visions unfortunately didn't stop at the arts, which would later factor into the Bauhaus' undoing. Great.

It was said that Gropius didn't know how to draw. This seemingly insignificant detail is, I believe, crucial to deciphering the source of the Bauhaus' influence, for had Gropius been a virtuoso architect (like Mies), the Bauhaus likely would never have been formed. Gropius was more of an ideas man, the rare individual who can assemble a diverse collection of talented people—which included the eccentric Johannes Itten who dressed like a monk—to work together toward a common goal. Gropius was the orchestra conductor, and this ability—not his design skills—was his special gift. Since it's likely been a hundred years since someone could get a group of academics to all pull in the same direction this, by itself, should be cause for celebration.

But the school never stood still for too long (perhaps a secret to its success). After four years, Gropius abruptly changed course, adopting a new focus on design for mass production: "Art into Industry" was the new motto (the monk would have to go). In this iteration, the designer would harness industrial technology and create well-designed, mass-produced goods. Hannes Meyer, Gropius' successor, took the school in a more overtly political direction, putting emphasis on "design for the masses" that would become one of the school's hallmarks but also get Meyer in hot water with the local authorities, who would turn to the apolitical Mies van der Rohe to reboot the school a third time.

If the Bauhaus owes its origin to Gropius, it owes its influence in the realm of architecture to Mies. He doubled down on the Bauhaus' emphasis on understanding materials, explaining "No design is possible until the materials with which you design are completely understood" and, like Josef Albers who focused on the limits of visual perception, stressed objectivity and a search for "truth" in an extra-moral sense. "Architecture, in my opinion," Mies would later say, "is not a subjective affair. The tendency should be in an objective direction." Subjectivity was for painters, not architects, according to Mies, so he re-drew the line between the arts and architecture that previous iterations of the Bauhaus had sought so assiduously to erase. The Bauhaus had become an architecture school.

The school was already famous by the time it was shut down by the National Socialists in 1933, enabling its faculty to emigrate across the globe to disseminate its teachings—Meyer to the Soviet Union, Albers to Black Mountain College and Gropius to Harvard's Graduate School of Design, where he promptly gave away the library because students shouldn't be looking at history books (you're welcome, Columbia). Ironically, the Nazis' attempt to destroy the Bauhaus only served to amplify its influence and ensure its legacy. Mies van der Rohe landed in Chicago at IIT, where his stripped-down Bauhaus approach found a welcome home in the no-nonsense Midwest metropolis. Mies' objective "solutions" to the "problem" of building turned out to be a smash hit with both developers and corporate America and were subsequently reproduced across the American landscape (but never improved upon), in the same way the German delicacy Hamburg steak became the ubiquitous hamburger here. Speaking in a lecture at the Blackstone Hotel in Chicago in 1953, twenty years after the Bauhaus closing, Mies was asked about the school's enduring impact:

"The fact that it [the Bauhaus] was an idea, I think, is the cause of the enormous influence the Bauhaus had on any progressive school around the world. You cannot do that with organization, you cannot do that with propaganda. Only an idea spreads so far." [1]

And spread it did. All great ideas eventually become a victim of their own success, their influence eventually so pervasive that it becomes invisible, and so it is with the Bauhaus. Architecture, its greatest beneficiary, for the most part has turned its back on Bauhaus doctrine and currently preoccupies itself with the kind of subjective self-expression and vacuous formalism that Mies and his Bauhaus colleagues abhorred. But elsewhere the principles of the Bauhaus live on today, hiding in plain sight. For it's in the iPhone that art meets technology and the Bauhaus ethos is fully realized—a product for the masses that is functional but beautiful, with clean lines, simplicity, and sophisticated use of advanced materials. It embodies the argument that everything can be improved through design. From the phone itself, to its packaging, advertising, to the design of the store in which it's sold, is it not a "total work of art" that Gropius (and Wagner) imagined?

Though in existence for a mere fourteen years, no school since has superseded the Bauhaus' global impact on architecture and design. But it's important to remember that it didn't begin as an architecture school, but grew out of an arts and crafts movement and ideas about the relationship between art and technology. Architecture wasn't added as a course of study until 1927. The Bauhaus evolved into an architecture school over time, and eventually transcended the field. It is likely that the next Bauhaus will emerge from an idea about technology, and come from somewhere other than architecture.

This essay was originally published in *Architectural Record*, June 2019.

In Conversation

Chicago

Clare Lyster: You've worked in Chicago for most of your career. What is it like to run a design practice in that city?

John Ronan: I think every place has its own DNA, a fundamental ethos or driving spirit encoded in its "bones," which forms its underlying character, and I believe as an architect that acknowledging and understanding a city's DNA is a precondition for making positive contributions to its culture. I would argue that Chicago's underlying spirit is a Midwestern pragmatism. You see this pragmatism reflected in the city's built environment and in the types of industries that call it home—insurance, financial services, and so on—and that make up its no-nonsense client base. The architects who succeed here are those who "crack the code" of this DNA and address the pragmatic but at the same time transcend it—like Mies van der Rohe, fowr example, whose buildings are very pragmatic and at the same time poetic and transcendent. And I would contend that Chicago's architectural reputation rests not on cultural buildings or monuments, as in other world-class cities, but on very ordinary building types: office buildings, schools, apartment buildings. So in my practice, I attempt to honor and extend this tradition of making the ordinary special.

Many designers who come to Chicago bemoan the pragmatism that prevails, thinking it prohibits design innovation.

Well, you can view it as a hindrance or as a catalyst. Look at all the great buildings this culture has produced! Innovation is possible here, but it typically arises out of the practical. At the end of the day, you cannot change the fundamental character of Chicago. You have to work within it and understand that you are part of a long cultural continuum that goes back to the Chicago School. I settled in Chicago because the culture aligned with my value system. I felt I belonged here. An architect needs to recognize what can and what can't be controlled. You can tinker with the cultural code but you are not going to change the fundamental character of a place. In a city as established as Chicago, the cultural context within which you work has a greater impact on you than you have on it. I urge my graduating students to make sure to locate themselves where the cultural DNA and their own value system align. Of course, that advice is predicated on *having* a value system.

How did the fact that you were building on the IIT campus designed by Mies van der Rohe and on a site near Crown Hall inform your design of the Innovation Center (Kaplan Institute)?

The two most architecturally significant campus plans in the U.S. are Mies's for IIT and Jefferson's for the University of Virginia. I wanted to respect IIT's tradition and at the same time design a building that was forward-looking and innovative—after all, I was designing an innovation center—but that felt like it belonged on the Mies campus. This requires you to walk a fine line. You want to make your own mark on the campus, but at the same time you must be respectful to the established order of an acknowledged master and be a steward of your cultural inheritance.

I proceeded very analytically, starting by examining the elements of the pre-established order that Mies laid down. For example, he designed the entire campus on a 24' grid, so we asked ourselves if that grid is still valid for today's buildings. To find out, we asked the faculty of IIT's Institute of Design, which was founded by Laszlo Moholy-Nagy and would be occupying the building, to provide us with paper sketches of their preferred classroom arrangements. The results confirmed that the grid works well, so we adopted it. Other elements of the Miesien vocabulary weren't so good. For example, because all the open space on campus is residual between the classroom boxes, there is no destination outdoor space on campus to sit down and have a cup of coffee. I thought our design should address that deficiency, which we did by adding internal courtyards to an overall building form that abides by the rules Mies established. We also asked ourselves if we should continue the use of steel frame that predominates on campus. Steel is still commonly used in the industry, so I have no problem adopting it, but I wanted our building to be more friendly and welcoming than the stern, Germanic buildings that Mies and SOM left behind. Our project is painted white and flooded with daylight, so it's bright and welcoming even on the cloudiest winter day. Creating a comfortable environment was a high priority because students and faculty spend their entire day in the Kaplan Institute, not an hour or two as they do in the adjacent classroom buildings.

Mies described his architecture as "skin and bones" and so I thought about what that might mean today. The ETFE (ethylene tetrafluoroethylene) is an obvious departure from the established

order of campus. I wanted to use a material that was not available to Mies, and I also wanted a very lightweight appearance for the building. Crown Hall was lightweight in appearance for its time, and I wanted to create a building that made Crown Hall look heavy by comparison. I wanted our building to be almost cloudlike, to seem as if it might float away were it not anchored to the ground.

We paid a great deal of attention to how we turned the ETFE corner because I knew that the architectural issue of *the corner* held great importance for Mies. We achieved our design, which is more reductive than the re-entrant variety he favored, by stretching the taut skin of the building around a clear acrylic rod, an innovation that hadn't yet been done elsewhere.

Themes

You say that your work is about relationships, not form. What do you mean by this?

The architecture I design needs to be experienced to be appreciated. Primarily, it is not about the *image* of the building but about space and how people move through it. I agree with Bruno Taut that Western architecture is about shape and form, and Asian architecture is about relationships. I feel a much greater affinity for the latter. I believe that too much contemporary architecture is about getting *noticed*, making visual one-liners that can be consumed in a single glance. My aim is to design buildings with richness and subtlety, that reward repeated experiencing and close attention. For example, the unfolding spatial quality of the Poetry Foundation building draws you in gradually.

It is conceived not as an object with a preferred viewing angle, but as a layered spatial composition of materials—wood, glass, zinc, and so on— which compress and separate to produce a spatial narrative. The visitor's experience moving through these layers constitutes the essence of the project. It is relational rather than formal. The individual layers that engender this spatial sequence are not special, in and of themselves; it is the interplay between and among them that is the source of the building's spatial qualities.

How has your idea of a "spatial narrative" evolved over the last ten years?

In one of my early projects, the winning competition entry for the Perth Amboy High School, in New Jersey (2004), the strategy was to create a field of ordinary rectangular volumes, clad in different materials, which slide and overlap to create a layered spatial quality. The strategy of the Gary Comer Youth Center (2006), which we were working on at the same time, is more interiorized, with overlapping bars of space tightly wound and centralized, producing a layering of interior space in which you can experience multiple spaces of the building simultaneously—you can be in one space and experience a second space through a third space. The project that followed, the Gary Comer College Prep (2010), was, in some ways, a precursor of the Poetry Foundation (2011) in the way in which the planes of the rainscreen facade depart the building volume to become space-defining elements. At the Poetry Foundation, the independent material planes separate and converge to create a subtle and complex layering of occupiable space and the interplay between the layers compounds the spatial effect—for example, the way the perforated zinc layer is reflected in the glass layer.

Why is contemporary architectural practice more focused on form than on space?

I think space has taken a back seat to form in our culture for a number of reasons. One is that advances in technology make it easier to design, document, fabricate, and construct complex forms, and architects are simply taking advantage of the opportunity that these new tools afford. Another reason is the way in which architecture is marketed and consumed in the media. It's much easier to sell and talk about the formally outrageous than the subtle. Space, character, atmosphere, and the more sensual aspects of architecture are more difficult to communicate. These parallel technological and media-driven developments have led to a prevailing "anything goes" environment in which the greatest sin is to be boring, but I think we architects need to ask ourselves, "What do we leave society when the novelty of form has worn off?"

Are there other underlying agendas that inform your work?

There is an intradisciplinary agenda that includes continuing to pursue the formally simple yet spatially complex. A related agenda concerns representation. If your values are in line with the more experiential aspects of architecture, how do you communicate that graphically, verbally, in models, and in writing?

I am interested in pursuing the influence of literature on architecture. Like a book, the building has a cover, a foreword, chapters that unfold one to the next, a climax, a conclusion, an afterword or coda. The Poetry Foundation building can be read in this way. And I subscribe to Umberto Eco's definition of the *modern*: a work that that is deliberately ambiguous and can be read in multiple ways. These are the qualities make a building modern, not its (orthogonal) geometry.

Another, more overarching, agenda concerns human dignity. There is an increasing willingness to sacrifice human dignity in favor of commercial and technological advancement. As I get older, I find myself foregrounding the restoration of dignity as a topic in the research phase of a project. South Shore High School, Independence Library and Apartments, and Chicago Park District Headquarters each attempt to arrest the trajectory toward expediency and degradation in public architecture. Many of the studio projects I give at IIT explore this question of human dignity.

Which historical or contemporary architects, artists, designers, or intellectuals do you align yourself with and why?

Among architects, Eero Saarinen, for his exploration of materiality and his ability to get to the essence of each project. Also, he didn't repeat himself, which is something that I strive for. I admire Sigurd Lewerentz for the idiosyncratic and timeless quality of his work, which looks like it could have been built hundreds of years ago or yesterday. Of architects practicing today, I admire Kazuyo Sejima for her diagrammatic clarity and originality and Christian Kerez for his war on the arbitrary and his ability to make a fresh architecture out of essential elements. The early work of Herzog de Meuron had a great influence on me, particularly their use of ordinary materials in an unconventional way and the way the building was a direct consequence of its construction.

I appreciate designer Jasper Morrison's ability to make traditional things new again and painter Brice Marden's exploration of irregular grids. His works on marble have informed my approach to adaptive reuse. Writer Kazuo Ishiguro's use of the structural devices of memory and perspective are illuminating for me. And poetry is especially valuable. It is about making the ordinary special, and the poet's process of choosing and sequencing ordinary words is analogous to making architecture. My favorite poets are Charles Simic for his originality and reductive purity, Billy Collins for his witty observations on the everyday, and Seamus Heaney for his lyricism and use of metaphor. As far as intellectuals go, I wish every architect would read French geographer Christophe Guilluy on globalization and gentrification; his work goes a long way towards explaining our current social ills.

What other values are important in architecture today?

I think the question of values is the most critical one facing architecture today. There once was general agreement across the profession on what questions architects should concern themselves with. Those days are gone. If we have learned anything in the past twenty years, it is that with enough capital and enough will, anything is possible. So, as an architect, what do you do when you can do anything? This reframes the question from "what *can* I do?" to "what *should* I do?" To answer this question, you must have a value system, and that is something every architect has to figure out, independently. For some, the priority is self-expression, for others, environmental stewardship. Many architects practicing today avoid the question of values entirely, which is why so much contemporary architecture looks arbitrary and vacuous. The architects who influenced me all have a clear value system that is legible in their work.

Office

You've chosen to keep your office small (never more than twenty people). Is this because you want to keep control, or have you concluded that this is the optimal size for a design practice?

It's both. Keeping the office small does have to do with maintaining control and staying close to the work throughout the process.

It allows us to be very nimble and responsive, qualities that enable me to establish the very close client relationships that I find crucial to doing high-quality work. As an office gets larger, this connection becomes tenuous and the work can suffer. Another reason for keeping things small is that I consider my office a "teaching office." I typically hire people directly out of school and train them to be architects, and I understand that the qualities I am after in my work require rigor and attention to detail that comes with experience and can't simply be delegated to junior team members.

Your office has become known for your institutional buildings, like the Poetry Foundation, the Gary Comer Youth Center, the Kaplan Institute at IIT, and the new Chicago Park District Headquarters, to name a few. Do you think institutional projects offer the best opportunity for putting into practice your idea of a "spatial narrative"?

The kinds of social interaction that happen in these buildings make them ideal for exploring the spatial ideas I'm interested in. The Kaplan Institute, for example, is intended to support interdisciplinary collaboration and chance meetings between faculty and students. Its spatially layered quality allows for visual access to multiple spaces simultaneously, which is critical to fostering a culture of collaboration. Seeing other people and the activities they are engaged in facilitates spontaneous engagement.

It is said that your work is a derivative of the modernist style because of its clean, elegant, orthogonal aesthetic. Do you agree? If so, what does it mean to operate within the language of modernism today?

I would say that my work employs modernist language but is not *about* that language, in the same way a novel written in English is rarely *about* the English language. Given that my work is more about communication than self-expression, I try to use a language that people understand. I don't feel the need to invent a new language or to adopt a personal set of opaque formal rules that refer back to me, which excludes the building user. I want people to focus on their experience with the building.

Context plays into this question. Chicago is laid out on an orthogonal grid, and is largely comprised of boxes placed on rectangular plots of land, so it is not surprising that most of the commissions I receive are for infill projects on rectangular lots, but I will take the opportunity to deviate from that paradigm when the situation calls for an object building. For example, a block-like building on the site chosen for the Obama Presidential Center would not be right, in my opinion. Depending on the given situation, certain established orders need to be confirmed, others need to be discarded or replaced, and it is the responsibility of the architect to discern the difference.

Pedagogy

In addition to your design practice, you are Professor of Architecture at the Illinois Institute of Technology (IIT). It's rare in this country to sustain an award-winning design practice that actually builds, along with an academic career that involves teaching, writing, and publishing. Such a combination is more common in Europe. Why do you think this is so unusual in the U.S.?

It's true that in the American system one is typically viewed as either a practitioner or an academic, and it's difficult to have credibility in both arenas. Few established academics have made successful career jumps to practices that build, and many academics regard teacher/practitioner colleagues more as studio instructors than as scholars. Straddling both worlds, you risk being dismissed by the academy as a mere practitioner, while in the market-driven world of the building industry you chance being written off as an impractical egghead. The practitioner/academic appeals to those rare clients who seek thoughtful architecture with an intellectual grounding. These clients exist; you just have to find them.

What do you teach at IIT, and what role does teaching play in your practice?

I teach upper-level design studios and seminars on the history and theory of material culture in architecture. You could say my practice is what I do, and my teaching is about how I think about what I do. Academia gives me the opportunity to research topics that I have not yet had the chance to explore through commissions. In my practice, I first formulate questions and topics that we can use the project to investigate. The work I do in that setting is more circumstantial and contingent than my work in academia, which is comparatively more abstract. You could say that in the office, I do research-based *design,* and at school, I do design-based *research*. Both are equally valid and mutually beneficial.

You were at Harvard's GSD in the late 1980s/early 1990s when Rafael Moneo was chair. How did the prevailing discourse influence your thinking?

It had a great impact. Moneo was a product of the European tradition of the practicing architect/academic that we just discussed, and his encyclopedic knowledge of the discipline served as a model for all of us. In retrospect, I suppose it is not merely coincidental that I followed the same path. It was a very critical environment. We were expected to develop a profound understanding of architectural history, and we faced rigorous interrogation by design juries. What I remember most is the clearly defined value system that pervaded the atmosphere. You were immersed in a shared school of thought premised on an architectural project you were implicitly buying into based on shared values. However, in the years since, architecture moved in a different direction— towards self-expression—and I believe a shared school of thought may no longer be possible.

This will be your third book. I find it interesting that some of the best-known architecture books have been written not by theoreticians but by practicing architects (Koetter and Rowe's Collage City; Venturi's Complexity and Contradiction; Rossi's Architecture of the City, come to mind). Is it important for architects to write? Does writing improve your practice?

Writing helps me clarify the thinking behind my work, which is easy to lose sight of when you are caught up in the day-to-day aspects of running a practice. The three publications you mention are all prescriptive, meaning that each was a kind of manifesto that would inform a body of work that was produced only later, after the book was written. That is not how it normally works, and it certainly doesn't work that way for me. I prefer the retrospective approach of Frank Lloyd Wright, who published the *Wasmuth Portfolio* only after he had spent a long time developing of his Prairie phase work. The *Portfolio* was a way of drawing conclusions and taking stock before moving on to something else. I've always thought that the way thesis is approached in architectural schools—a semester of writing prior to the design project— is backwards. One should do the design first and then write about it. In practice, design precedes theory. The examples you cite are famous in part because they are notable exceptions. Most architects who write don't think of their work in this prescriptive, didactic way.

Writing about architecture is a way to unburden myself, of getting something out so that I can move on to new things. What I write is more like a memoir than a treatise. Writing also serves as an outlet for thoughts that a building project is powerless to communicate.

It's important to understand that nobody likes to write—not even writers. A well-regarded novelist once told me, "I write when the thought of not writing the book becomes more painful than writing the book." I can sympathize with that. Writing can be difficult, but it's a good way of figuring out where you've been, what you've learned. And what you write might help someone else.

What do you imagine architecture will be like in twenty-five years?

I think certain trends already underway will continue. The profession will become increasingly specialized, and the generalist architect will become a figure from the past, replaced by specialists, similar to the evolution of the medical field. Even now, multiple architecture firms will work on the same project the way doctors work on a patient, one giving the building its outward form, another designing the interior layout, and another focusing on the technical aspects. It's not hard to see where this leads and the results won't always be good. I also think that the trend toward ever larger firms will continue, and in the future you will see fewer, but much larger, organizations setting up branches in cities large and small, which will have a homogenizing effect on architectural production. Developments in computer software will only compound these homogenizing forces. At some point, we will become so saturated with sameness that a rebellion against it will be unleashed, as happened in the food world with the rise of farm-to-table and locally grown movements. Ultimately, people crave authenticity, something with a story.

Chronology

1999

The office of John Ronan Architect formed

Winner, Townhouse Revisited Competition, Graham Foundation for Advanced Studies in the Fine Arts

Townhouse Revisited Exhibition, Graham Foundation, Chicago Illinois

209 East Lake Shore Drive Residence

John Ronan named Adjunct Professor at Illinois Institute of Technology College of Architecture

2000

Coach House

11 Woodley Road Residence

Redsquared

513 North Walcott Residence

428 West Webster Residence

Chapel in the Woods

Catholic Extension Chapel

2001

Todd Hase Showroom

House on the Edge of a Forest

541 West Belden

Chicago Public Schools Competition

Comma Music

2002

Catfish Music

Tiffiny Decorating Co.

ING Trading Office

Speculative Chicago Exhibition, Gallery 400, University of Illinois at Chicago

2003

John Ronan named Assistant Professor at the Illinois Institute of Technology College of Architecture

Akiba-Schechter Jewish Day School (Phase One)

Sabbia Jewelry Store

67 East Bellevue Residence

Precast Concrete Affordable Housing

Perth Amboy High School

Precast Chapel

Old Post Office

2004

Winner, Perth Amboy High School Design Competition, February 2004

Perth Amboy High School Design Competition Exhibition, The Architectural League of New York, New York

House on the Lake

Visionary Chicago Architecture Exhibition, Graham Foundation, Chicago, Illinois

Big & Green Chicago Exhibition, The Chicago Architecture Foundation, Chicago, Illinois

2005

P/A Award Citation, Perth Amboy High School

52nd Annual P/A Awards Exhibition, Center for Architecture, New York, New York

Chicago Square, Hafencity, Hamburg Germany

Long Bay Villas (Anguilla)

Chicago Line Vessel

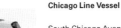

South Chicago Avenue Streetscaping

2006

    Akiba-Schechter Jewish Day School
    (Phase Two)

    Concrete Townhouse

    Gary Comer Youth Center

    3020 Lake Shore Drive Residence

    Herman Miller Classics

    *Perth Amboy High School Design
    Competition* Exhibition, Cornell University
    School of Architecture, Ithaca, New York

    Young Chicago Exhibition, The Art Institute
    of Chicago, Chicago, Illinois

2007

    CMK Offices

    South Caicos Masterplan

    Chicago 2016 Olympics Bid, Live Site
    and Archery Venue

    Urban Model High Schools

    Ten Box House

2008

    John Ronan named Associate Professor
    at Illinois Institute of Technology College
    of Architecture

    Yale Steam Laundry

    Loft House

    Lock Rum Villas, Anguilla

    Glencoe Residence

    South Caicos Villas & Condominiums

    South Caicos Beach Club

2009

    American Institute of Architects
    National Honor Award for Architecture,
    Gary Comer Youth Center

    Courtyard House

    House in Three Parts

    Desert House

2010

    Gary Comer College Prep School

    **Christ the King Jesuit College
    Preparatory School**

    South Shore High School

    Kelly Curie Gage Park Area High School

    *Explorations: The Architecture of John
    Ronan* published by Princeton
    Architectural Press

2011

    Poetry Foundation

    IIT Smart Grid Training Center

    ***Bertrand Goldberg: Architect of Invention,
    Exhibition Design, Art Institute of Chicago***

    Manufactured Housing Prototype

    American Institute of Architects/Committee
    on Architecture for Education Educational
    Facility Design Awards Program, Award of
    Merit, Gary Comer College Prep,
    AIA National

    Rudy Bruner Award for Urban Excellence,
    Silver Medalist, Gary Comer Youth Center/
    Gary Comer College Prep

    Design on the Edge Exhibition, The Chicago
    Architecture Foundation, Chicago, Illinois

2012

American Institute of Architects National Honor Award for Architecture, Poetry Foundation

Grand Crossing Master Plan

Societe Privee de Gerance Office Building

Encodings: The Work of John Ronan Architects Exhibition, Roger Williams University, Bristol, Rhode Island

2013

860 Lake Shore Drive Residence

Veterans Affordable Housing

Erie Elementary Charter School

Iterations: John Ronan's Poetry Foundation Exhibition, The Art Institute of Chicago, Chicago, Illinois

2014

Jefferson Park Masterplan

Ed Paschke Art Center

880 Lake Shore Drive Residence

2015

University Conference Center, Invited Competition, University of Chicago

Leaf Lounge, Chicago Architecture Biennial (inaugural)

The Poetry Foundation published by Centerline Press, Center for American Architecture and Design, University of Texas at Austin

2016

Blu Dot

Tastyworks

Obama Presidential Center, Invited Competition

2017

American Academy of Arts and Letters Architecture Award Winner, John Ronan

Courtyard House

R + D Award, Architect magazine, IIT Innovation Center Dynamic ETFE Façade American Academy of Arts and Letters 2017 Architecture Award Winner, John Ronan

American Academy of Arts and Letters Architecture Award Exhibition, American Academy of Arts and Letters, New York, New York

2018

John Ronan named Distinguished Professor by Association of College Schools of Architecture

Gallery House

151 North Franklin

John Ronan named John G. Williams Visiting Professor in Architecture, University of Arkansas

Illinois Institute of Technology Innovation Center (Kaplan Institute)

Brick by Brick, Word by Word published in Poetry Magazine

860-880 Lake Shore Drive Essay published in *Chicago by the Book,* University of Chicago Press

University College Dublin Future Campus and Centre for Creative Design, Invited Competition

Kedzie Terminal

John Ronan awarded the John and Jeanne Rowe Endowed Chair Professorship of the College of Architecture, Illinois Institute of Technology

352

Independence Library and Apartments

The Acres Gallery

Erie Serpent Pedestrian Bridge

American Institute of Architects National Innovation Award, Illinois Institute of Technology Innovation Center (Kaplan Institute)

American Institute of Architects/Committee on Architecture for Education National Education Facility Design Award, Illinois Institute of Technology Innovation Center (Kaplan Institute)

Lemont Pedestrian Bridge (in design)

Hyde Park Neighborhood Club (in design)

American Institute of Architects Housing Award, Independence Library and Apartments

Noble Fieldhouse (in design)

880 Lake Shore Drive Residence (in construction)

Evanston Compound (in design)

North Side Cultural District/ Ed Paschke Art Center (in design)

University of Pittsburgh Forbes Avenue Building (in design)

Chicago Park District Headquarters (in construction)

Lemont Quarries Adventure Park (in design)

Frank Lloyd Wright Home and Studio Museum Learning Center (in design)

University of Cincinnati Alumni Center (in design)

Wildwood Cabin (in design)

Bloomfield Civic Center/Library/Affordable Housing

Arena Park, Invited Competition

American Institute of Architects National Honor Award for Architecture, Illinois Institute of Technology Innovation Center (Kaplan Institute)

American Institute of Architects/American Library Association National Library Building Award, Independence Library

Athenaum Center for Thought and Culture (in construction)

Acknowledgements

Anyone who undertakes a building project has my admiration. Buildings are expensive propositions and their design and realization is a long, complicated process. Commissioning one requires courage and perseverance, so I will begin by thanking the clients who have placed their trust and faith in me over the years.

I would like to offer special thanks John and Jeanne Rowe, whose endowed chair I hold at the Illinois Institute of Technology College of Architecture. Many in their position choose to reward success, using their influence to support wealthy institutions as a form of personal validation. Others go where they are needed, and the Rowe's are in this latter category. I am honored to call them friends and grateful for their generosity and support—both of the university and of me, personally.

I have had the good fortune to work with many talented people over the years in my studio. I consider my firm a "teaching office" and the vast majority of people who have worked in my studio over the years I hired directly out of architecture school. This book is a testament to their optimism, enthusiasm, talent, hard work and dedication. I hope it triggers a sense of pride and stirs up fond memories of their time in the studio.

I know no one in architecture more perspicacious than the gifted architect, writer and critic Carlos Jiminez, and I am honored to have him write an essay on my work. I first met Carlos when presenting our Perth Amboy High School design competition scheme, for which he served as jury member. I was stunned by his insight, thoughtful analysis of the scheme and the poetry with which he delivered his comments.

I would like to thank my friend and IIT colleague Sean Keller for his contribution to the book. I knew that whatever Sean would write about my work would be of enduring value to me, that I would learn something about architecture and myself, and I was not disappointed.

354

I am indebted to Clare Lyster for her understanding of the value of the interview format in explaining an architect's work, and I thank her for asking all the right questions to properly position the studio's work and unearth its intellectual and conceptual underpinnings.

Making a book is like making a building—there is much research, thought and effort that factor into its realization, involving numerous individuals. I thank my studio colleague Eric Cheng, who was instrumental in assembling the visual materials for the book, and whose discerning eye was invaluable in reviewing its numerous drafts, graphic layouts and image crops. Rick Valicenti made sure that the design of the book aligned with the value system of the studio, and I thank him for his creativity and guidance; special thanks goes to Anna Mort for her talent, dedication and attention to detail in the book's graphic design. I would also like to acknowledge copy editor Susan Miller, who was instrumental in keeping the prose concise and on point and, finally, the folks at Actar—Marga, Ramon and Ricardo—who guided us through the process.

Biographies

Sean Keller is a historian and critic of modern and contemporary architecture. He is the author of *Automatic Architecture: Motivating Form After Modernism* (University of Chicago Press, 2018) and has written for numerous anthologies and journals. His work has been recognized by a Warhol Foundation Grant and a Winterhouse Award for Design Writing and Criticism. His next book, on the architecture, art, and landscape of the 1972 Olympics in Munich, is forthcoming from Yale University Press.

Sean Keller is associate professor and associate dean at the IIT College of Architecture. He has taught at Harvard University, Yale University, and at the University of Chicago, where he has been a fellow of both the Neubauer Collegium and the Franke Institute for the Humanities. He is a trustee of the Graham Foundation. He holds a PhD from Harvard University and MArch and BA degrees from Princeton University.

Clare Lyster is an architect and founding principal of CLUAA, a research-based design office in Chicago that explores the design of the built environment from the perspective of urban systems and emerging socio-technical networks. She is the author of *Learning from Logistics: How Networks Change Cities* (Birkhäuser, 2016), which focuses on how contemporary digital platforms transform urban space, and coeditor of *Third Coast Atlas: Prelude to a Plan* (Actar, 2017), which explores the relationship between urbanization and hydrology in the Great Lakes Region of North America. She is cocurator with ANNEX of *Entanglement*, the Irish pavilion at the 2021 Venice Architecture Biennale, which investigates the material imprint of data technologies, and coeditor of an eponymous publication to be published by Actar in 2021. She is the recipient of the 2017 Douglas Gillmor Visiting Lectureship at the University of Calgary, the 2019–21 University of Illinois at Chicago (UIC) CADA Distinguished Faculty Award, the 2019 UIC Distinguished Scholar Award in Art, Architecture and the Humanities, and the 2019 SOM Foundation Research Prize. She is an associate professor in the School of Architecture at UIC.

Carlos Jimenez was born in San José, Costa Rica in 1959. He moved to the United States in 1974 and graduated in 1981 from the University of Houston School of Architecture, where he received awards for best thesis project and best portfolio. He established his own office in Houston in 1983. He is a tenured professor at Rice University School of Architecture since 2000 and has received multiple awards for his teaching excellence, including Design Intelligence Most Admired Educator, in 2013. He has held numerous visiting professorships, including at the University of Texas at Austin and Harvard University and has served as lecturer, juror and visiting critic at universities and cultural institutions throughout the Americas, Europe, the Middle East, and Japan. Carlos served as jury member of the Pritzker Architecture Prize from 2001-2011. His work has been exhibited in galleries throughout North and South America and been the subject of four publications and featured extensively in the international design press.

John Ronan FAIA is founding principal and lead designer of John Ronan Architects, in Chicago. He is known for his abstract yet sensuous work exploring materiality and atmosphere. John holds an MArch with distinction from the Harvard University Graduate School of Design and a BS from the University of Michigan. His work has been exhibited internationally and extensively covered by the design press and is the subject of two previous publications. He has lectured widely, and his writing has appeared in books, architecture journals, and *Poetry* magazine. John Ronan Architects has garnered numerous national and international design awards, including three AIA National Architecture Awards. In 2017, John received the American Academy of Arts and Letters Architecture Award. He has been visiting chair at numerous universities and is currently the John and Jeanne Rowe Endowed Chair Professor of Architecture at the Illinois Institute of Technology College of Architecture where he has taught since 1992.

Project Credits

The Old Post Office (2003)
Location: Chicago, Illinois
Client: Chicago Central Area Committee
Project team: John Ronan, Micah Land

Perth Amboy High School (2003–2004)
Location: Perth Amboy, New Jersey
Client: New Jersey Schools Construction Corporation
Project team: John Ronan, Brian Malady, Yasushi Koakutsu,
Brad Kelley, Micah Land, Oscar Kang
Consultants: Arup (structural)

The Gary Comer Youth Center (2004–2006)
Location: Chicago, Illinois
Client: Comer Science and Education Foundation
Project team: John Ronan, Brian Malady, Evan Menk, Brad Kelley,
Yasushi Koakutsu, Oscar Kang, Nageshwar Rao, Micah Land
Consultants: Arup (structural); CCJM Engineers (mepfp);
Terra Engineering (civil); Peter Lindsay Schaudt Landscape
Architecture (landscape); Kirkegaard Associates (acoustics);
Shuler & Shook (theatrical); Charter Sills (lighting)
Builder: W. E. O'Neil Construction
Photography: Steve Hall, Chris Lake, Jasmin Shah, Wes Pope

Yale Steam Laundry (2005–2008)
Location: Washington, DC
Client: IBG Partners/Greenfield Partners
Project team: John Ronan, Brian Malady, Brad Kelley, Yasushi
Koakutsu, Oscar Kang, Sonja Mueller
Consultants: BBGM (architect of record); Holbert Apple Associates
(structural); GHT Limited (mepfp); Charter Sills (lighting)
Builder: Clark Construction
Photography: Nathan Kirkman

Gary Comer College Prep (2008–2010)
Location: Chicago, Illinois
Client: Comer Science and Education Foundation
Project team: John Ronan, Josh Bergman, Evan Menk, Marcin Szef,
Anna Ninoyu, Sam Zeller
Consultants: Goodfriend Magruder Structure, LLC (structural);
WMA Consulting Engineers (mepfp); Terra Engineering (civil);
Hoerr Schaudt Landscape Architects (landscape);
Kirkegaard Associates (acoustics, a/v)
Builder: Norcon, Inc.
Photography: Steve Hall, Jasmin Shah

The Poetry Foundation (2007–2011)
Location: Chicago, Illinois
Client: The Poetry Foundation
Project team: John Ronan, Evan Menk, Tom Lee, John Trocke,
Wonwoo Park
Consultants: Arup (structural); dbHMS (mepfp); Terra Engineering
(civil); Reed/Hilderbrand (landscape); Threshold Acoustics
(acoustics); Sako Associates (security); Anders Dahlgren (library);
Charter Sills (lighting)
Builder: Norcon
Photography: Steve Hall, James Florio, Bill Zbaren,
Francisco Lopez De Arenosa

Erie Elementary Charter School (2011–2013)
Location: Chicago, Illinois
Client: Erie Elementary Charter School
Project team: John Ronan, Evan Menk, Marcin Szef, Josh Bergman,
Tom Lee
Consultants: Goodfriend Magruder (structural); dbHMS (mepfp);
Terra Engineering (civil); Primera (sustainability)
Builder: Norcon
Photography: Steve Hall

Courtyard House (2013–2017)
Location: Saint Joseph, Michigan
Client: Jody and Brad Kapnick
Project team: John Ronan, Marcin Szef, Eric Cheng,
Danielle Beaulieu
Consultants: Goodfriend Magruder Structure LLC (structural);
dbHMS (mepfp)
Builder: Michael Wood
Photography: Steve Hall

Gallery House (2015–2017)
Location: Chicago, Illinois
Client: Tony and Robin Armour
Project team: John Ronan, Sam Park, Laura Gomez Hernandez
Consultants: Stearn-Joglekar (structural); AA Service (mechanical)
Builder: Fraser Construction
Photography: Tony Armour

151 North Franklin (2012–2018)
Location: Chicago, Illinois
Client: The John Buck Company
Project team: John Ronan, Marcin Szef, Sam Park, Eric Cheng,
Laura Gomez Hernandez
Consultants: Adamson Associates Architects (architect of record);
Magnusson Klemencic Associates (structural); Environmental
Systems Design, Inc. (mepfp); Mackie Consultants (civil);
Wolff Landscape Architecture (landscape); Shiner Acoustics
(acoustics); Aurora Lighting Design (lighting); Jenkins &
Huntington (vertical transportation)
Builder: Lend Lease
Photography: Steve Hall

The Ed Kaplan Family Institute for Innovation and Tech Entrepreneurship (2014–2018)
Location: Chicago, Illinois
Client: Illinois Institute of Technology
Project team: John Ronan, Marcin Szef, Danielle Beaulieu, Eric Cheng, Sam Park, Laura Gomez Hernandez
Consultants: Werner Sobek (structural); dbHMS (mepfp, sustainability); Terra Engineering (civil); Terry Guen Design Associates (landscape); Charter Sills (lighting); Jenson Hughes (security); Thirst (interior graphics)
Builder: Power Construction Company
Photography: Steve Hall, James Florio

University Conference Center (2015)
Location: Chicago, Illinois
Client: University of Chicago
Project team: John Ronan, Marcin Szef, Sam Park, Eric Cheng, Danielle Beaulieu, Laura Gomez Hernandez
Consultants: Werner Sobek (structural); dbHMS (mepfp); Terra Engineering (civil); Michael Boucher Landscape Architecture (landscape); Atelier Ten (sustainability)

The Obama Presidential Center (2016)
Location: Chicago, Illinois
Client: Obama Foundation
Project team: John Ronan, Marcin Szef, Sam Park, Eric Cheng, Danielle Beaulieu, Laura Gomez Hernandez, Brett Gustafson, Andrew Akins
Consultants: Thornton Tomasetti (structural); dbHMS (mepfp); Atelier Ten (sustainability); Michael Boucher Landscape Architecture (landscape)

University of Cincinnati Alumni Center (2017–present)
Location: Cincinnati, Ohio
Client: University of Cincinnati
Project team: John Ronan, Marcin Szef, Sam Park, Eric Cheng, Danielle Beaulieu, Laura Gomez Hernandez, John Kerner, Wenda Wei
Consultants: Thornton Tomasetti (structural); dbHMS (mepfp)

University College Dublin Future Campus and Centre for Creative Design (2018)
Location: Belfield, Dublin, Ireland
Client: University College Dublin
Project team: John Ronan, Marcin Szef, Eric Cheng, Sam Park, John Kerner, Wenda Wei, Courtney Arabea, Philip Syvertsen, Weilun Chen
Consultants: Arup Dublin (structural, civil, transport planning); CLUAA (urban design); Michael Boucher Landscape Architecture (landscape); Transsolar (sustainability); RKD (associate architect)

Lemont Quarries Adventure Park (2018–present)
Location: Lemont, Illinois
Client: The Forge
Project team: John Ronan, Marcin Szef, Sam Park, John Kerner, Courtney Arabea, Maranda Gerga
Consultants: Thornton Tomasetti (structural); Affiliated Engineers (mepfp, IT, lighting, security, sustainability); Terra Engineering (civil); Site Design Group (landscape); Hey and Associates (ecological); Shen Milsom & Wilke (acoustics, a/v)

Independence Library and Apartments (2017–2019)
Location: Chicago, Illinois
Client: Evergreen Real Estate
Project team: John Ronan, Marcin Szef, Andrew Akins, Will Corcoran, Sam Park, Eric Cheng, Danielle Beaulieu, John Kerner, Wenda Wei, Courtney Arabea
Consultants: Thornton Tomasetti (structural); dbHMS (mepfp, lighting, sustainability); Terra Engineering (civil, landscape); Shiner Acoustics (acoustics)
Builder: Leopardo Companies
Photography: James Florio

Frank Lloyd Wright Home and Studio Museum Learning Center (2018–present)
Location: Oak Park, Illinois
Client: Frank Lloyd Wright Trust
Project team: John Ronan, Eric Cheng, Courtney Arabea, Sepideh Merikhipour, Maranda Gerga
Consultants: Goodfriend Magruder (structural); dbHMS (mepfp); Terra Engineering (civil)
Builder: Bulley & Andrews

Chicago Park District Headquarters (2019–2022)
Location: Chicago, Illinois
Client: Chicago Park District
Project team: John Ronan, Marcin Szef, Sam Park, Eric Cheng, John Kerner, Courtney Arabea, Philip Syvertsen, Maranda Gerga
Consultants: Thornton Tomasetti (structural); dbHMS (mepfp); Terra Engineering (civil); Site Design Group (landscape); Shen Milsom & Wilke (acoustics, a/v, security); Charter Sills (lighting)
Builder: F.H. Paschen

Out of the Ordinary
the work of John Ronan Architects

Published by
Actar Publishers, New York, Barcelona
www.actar.com

Author
John Ronan

Edited by
Actar Publishers

Graphic Design
Rick Valicenti
Anna Mort

With contributions by
Carlos Jimenez
Sean Keller
Clare Lyster

Copy editing
Susan Miller

Printing and binding
Arlequin

Distribution
Actar D, Inc. New York, Barcelona.

New York
440 Park Avenue South, 17th Floor
New York, NY 10016, USA
salesnewyork@actar-d.com

Barcelona
Roca i Batlle 2
08023 Barcelona, Spain
eurosales@actar-d.com

Indexing
English ISBN: 978-1-63840-978-6
Library of Congress Control Number: 2021943728

Printed in Spain

Publication date: January 2022

Cover image: James Florio